FAREWELL TO EDEN

Farewell to EDEN

MATTHEW HUXLEY
CORNELL CAPA

HARPER & ROW Publishers
New York and Evanston

FAREWELL TO EDEN

Text: MATTHEW HUXLEY

Photographs and photographic editing: CORNELL CAPA

Design: CHARLOTTE TROWBRIDGE DYER

FIRST EDITION

Library of Congress Catalog Card Number: 64-20546

Other photographs in this book are by linguists Robert Russell, Willard Kindberg, Lambert Anderson, and Robert Tripp of Wycliffe Bible Translators; and by Samuel Milbank and Robert Carneiro.

Printed by Conzett and Huber in Zurich, Switzerland, for Harper & Row, Publishers, 1964, through Chanticleer Press, Inc., New York.

CONTENTS

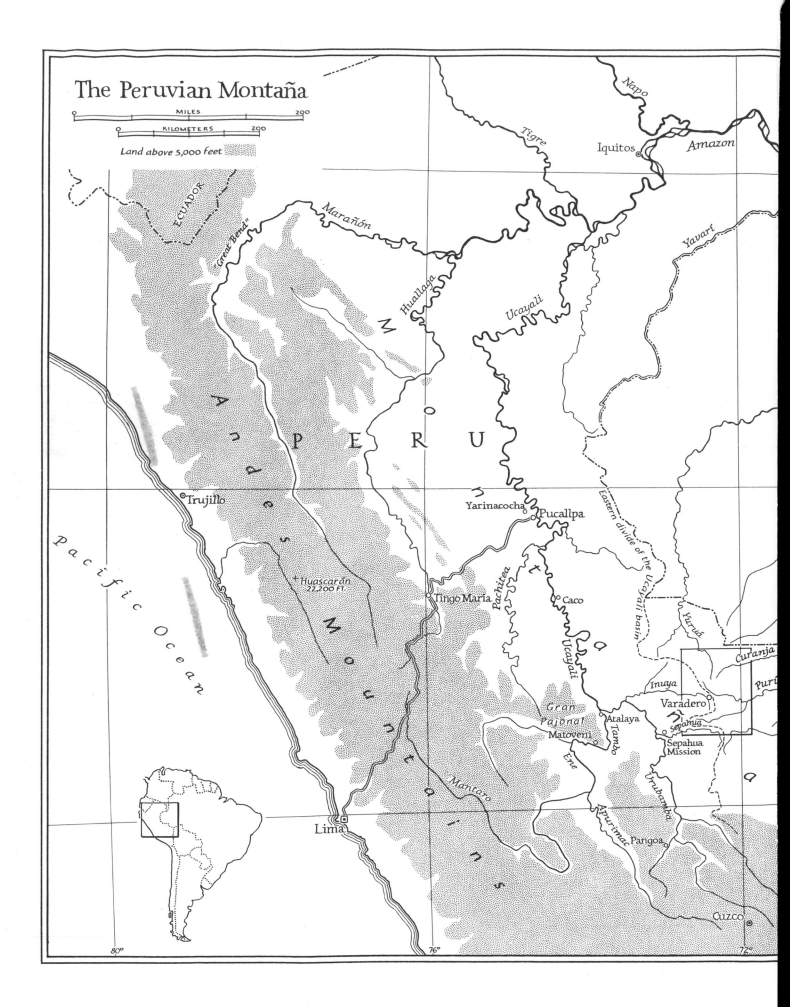

The Peruvian Montaña

MILES 200
KILOMETERS 200

Land above 5,000 feet

Napo

Tigre

Marañón

Iquitos

Amazon

ECUADOR

"Great Bend"

Yavari

Huallaga

M

Ucayali

Trujillo

Yarinacocha · Pucallpa

P E R U

Eastern divide of the Ucayali basin

o

+ Huascarán
22,200 FT.

Pachitea

Tingo María

Caco

u

Juruá

Curanja

Purú

n

Ucayali

Inuya

Pacific Ocean

t

Varadero

a

Gran
Pajonal

Sepahua

Atalaya

Matoveni

Tambo

Sepahua
Mission

i

Ene

Urubamba

Mantaro

n

s

Apurimac Pangoa

Lima

Cuzco

80°   76°   72°

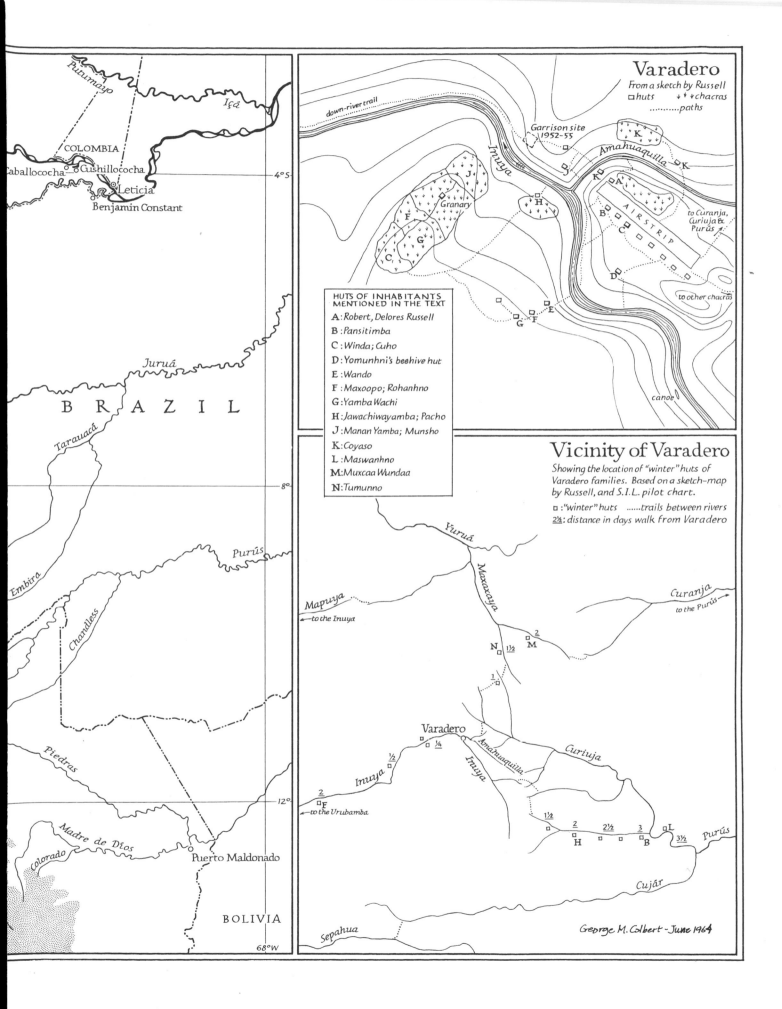

Varadero
From a sketch by Russell
□ huts   ↓ ↑ chacras
.........paths

down-river trail

Garrison site
1952-55

Inuya

Amahuaquilla

K

J

J

K

K

H

A

Granary

F

B

AIRSTRIP

to Curanja,
Curiuja &
Purús

C

G

D

C

to other chacras

F

E

G

canoe

HUTS OF INHABITANTS
MENTIONED IN THE TEXT
A: Robert, Delores Russell
B: Pansitimba
C: Winda; Cuho
D: Yomunhni's beehive hut
E: Wando
F: Maxoopo; Rohanhno
G: Yamba Wachi
H: Jawachiwayamba; Pacho
J: Manan Yamba; Munsho
K: Coyaso
L: Maswanhno
M: Muxcaa Wundaa
N: Tumunno

COLOMBIA

Putumayo

Içá

Caballococha — Cushillococha

Leticia

Benjamin Constant

4° S

Juruá

BRAZIL

Tarauacá

Purús

Embira

Chandless

Piedras

Madre de Dios

Colorado

Puerto Maldonado

BOLIVIA

8°

12°

68° W

Vicinity of Varadero
*Showing the location of "winter" huts of
Varadero families. Based on a sketch-map
by Russell, and S.I.L. pilot chart.*

□ : "winter" huts   .....trails between rivers
2½ : distance in days walk from Varadero

Yuruá

Maxaxaya

Curanja

Mapuya

to the Inuya

to the Purús

N   1½

2
M

1

Varadero

¼

Amahuaquilla

Curiuja

Inuya

½

Inuya

2
F

to the Urubamba

1½

2
H

2½

3
B

L

3½

Purús

Cujár

Sepahua

George M. Colbert - June 1964

Acknowledgments

In acknowledgment of our great debt to Mr. Samuel R. Milbank we dedicate this book. Without him this record of a vanishing culture could not have been made, and it is our hope that he will accept this volume as repayment in some small measure for his concern.

To Dr. Gertrude Dole and Dr. Robert Carneiro, Department of Anthropology of the American Museum of Natural History, our debt is vast. We were able to mine unique data contained in their Amahuaca field notes. More importantly, they gave us their professional judgment, unfailing kindness and encouragement.

We are equally obligated to Mr. and Mrs. Robert Russell of the Summer Institute of Linguistics. We quartered ourselves upon them for weeks at a time, and impressed Mr. Russell as official cameraman and historian of the Amahuaca. Without his help it would have been impossible to make so complete a record of the tribe.

Our thanks, too, go to the Summer Institute of Linguistics, Peruvian Branch, who made us so warmly welcome, and who offered us the total range of their skills and knowledge. We are indebted to many of its members, in particular to Mr. and Mrs. Lambert Anderson, Mr. Kenneth Kensinger, Mr. and Mrs. Willard Kindberg, Miss Esther Matteson, Mr. and Mrs. Wesley Thiesen, Mr. Robert Tripp, and other field linguists and staff members for information about the tribes they work with; and to the many supporting staff who frequently filled our peculiar needs. And last, since they are first, to Dr. William Cameron Townsend and his wife Elaine go our best wishes for the continued success of the great venture.

Finally, a deep and very personal sense of gratitude is due Frank G. Boudreau, M.D., who did so much to encourage the writer, then a member of his staff.

M.H. and C.C.
April 1964

Introduction

IN THE SUMMER OF 1961 Cornell Capa and I journeyed some thirty-five hundred miles due south of New York City on a trip that was to take us back thirty-five hundred years in time. Within one week of leaving a megalopolis of seventeen million people, we settled into Puesto Varadero, a jungle community of seventeen families on the Peruvian-Brazilian border, to begin this record of a Stone Age culture.

Twenty years ago Varadero did not exist, and even today you will have a hard time finding this tiny settlement on any except the most recent and large-scale maps. Yet small as it is, it is almost certainly the largest community of Amahuaca* Indians in existence within the tropical jungles of Peru; and the Amahuaca, a Panoan-speaking group, have probably had less to do with the white man than any other tribe of the Montaña, as the Peruvian section of the Amazon jungle is called. It is safe to say that the group at Varadero has met no more than a couple of dozen whites within its collective memory.

In the Amahuaca culture we can identify many traits that will be found elaborated amongst the other tribes of the area. This is certainly true insofar as the mechanics of extracting a living from the jungle are concerned. For regardless of tribe or linguistic group, whether living in the north or south of the Montaña or settled on big rivers or small streams, the Montaña Indian, until a century ago, lived off the jungle in quite the same way as the Amahuaca do today.

This is true, too, of the Amahuaca's primitive social organization—and compared to some of the other tribes of the Montaña, the Amahuaca are socially very primitive indeed.

For example, murder amongst the more socially developed Montaña tribes was organized into intervillage raids and intertribal wars; the frequent murders and vendettas amongst the Amahuaca are individual affairs. Infanticide, in a number of the Montaña tribes, is socially required under certain conditions; an

---

* A guide to pronouncing Amahuaca names will be found in the back of this book.

Amahuaca mother will murder a newborn simply because she feels she would be overburdened by it. When compared with the ritual cannibalism that was so central to the social life of many Panoan Montaña tribes, the endocannibalism of the Amahuaca has a very primitive aspect.

Marriage and the sexual mores of the Amahuaca are another example of their simple social organization. In order to reinforce group and tribal solidarity, most Montaña tribes have elaborated social structures that require marriages to cross moiety (clan) lines. In contrast, the only functioning social unit amongst the Amahuaca is the family. Solidarity, therefore, is maintained by permitting complete sexual freedom between a man's wife and all his brothers, and by fostering cross-cousin marriages to avoid sister-brother and father-daughter unions. In short, the Amahuaca can be considered as a "dehydrated" version of much of the Indian culture of the area before the white man came.

What we found at Varadero was a Stone Age agricultural society in process of transformation. For the lives of these Amahuaca are being changed: the world outside their jungle is creeping in on them, and their primitive culture is being modified.

This book, then, is a record in some detail of a way of life that will inevitably vanish—a record of how the Amahuaca live and look and think; how they view the world around them; how, in turn, this world of theirs is changing. It is also an attempt to speculate on the fate of the Amahuaca when they enter the mainstream of Montaña life.

Their prospects seem dim indeed. Relegated to the bottom of society, as Western man regards it, the Indian rapidly develops a desperate desire to lose his tribal identity and replace it with that of the white man. This appears the only way out of his abysmal position.

However, the process almost certainly assures his cultural extinction. Whether he becomes a debt-entrapped serf or a wretched day laborer, he is reduced to something less than a man, both in his own eyes and in those of his society.

A number of agencies try to save the Indian from this fate. Some attempt to solve his problem by making him a complete Peruvian, sending him forth into the Montaña with new skills and a new identity. Others attempt, with varying degrees of success, to preserve his identity by giving him pride in his Indian tradition.

The problem is to maintain the Indian's tribal identity and hence his self respect, while teaching him a new technology so that he can become a respected member of the dominant society.

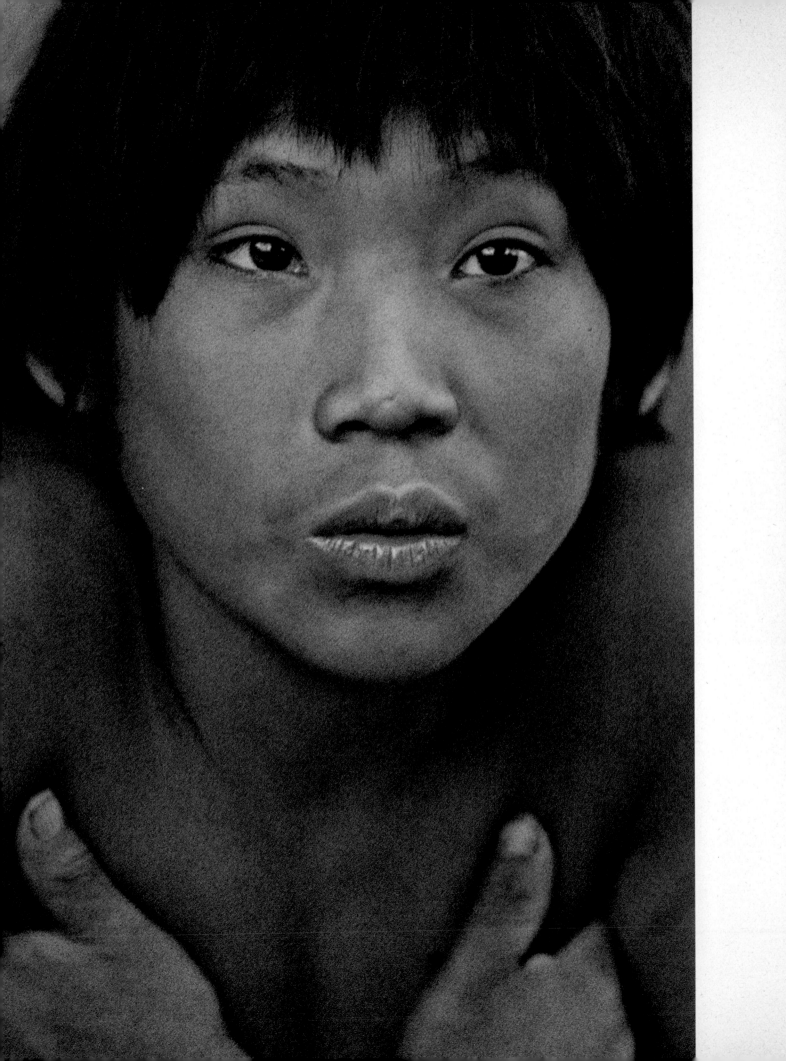

I

I ARRIVE AT VARADERO WITH A BANG or, more exactly, in a drum roll of bangs: the airstrip is but a hundred and fifty yards long, and the only plane that can get in and out is a Helio Courier. The jungle, a dull gray-green from three thousand feet above, comes to life as the dense canopy below resolves into individual trees and branches. We bounce heavily down the field, and skid to a halt forty yards from the dense wall of jungle. The motor is gunned to a roar, and we taxi back to the six huts at the bottom of the field, jouncing past a border of bananas, pineapples, and bamboo.

Waiting by the biggest hut are about a dozen people, and as they crowd around the plane I'm startled at how red they are, how small they seem, how naked the men in their marvelous top hats. The Amahuaca appear a handsome lot: the women boldly featured, handsomely endowed; the men reminiscent of Renaissance drawings demonstrating the classic proportions of the human body. Sand-bagged by the heat and the intense brightness of the noonday sun, I envy the Indians their undress, for the women wear only a short sheath skirt rolled about their waists, while the men go quite naked with the exception of a bark belt into which they tuck their foreskins.

Hanging back from the first rush of Amahuaca are ethnologists Robert Carneiro and Gertrude Dole, the husband-and-wife team with whom I shall be staying. They are from the American Museum of Natural History, and have been living quite by themselves at Varadero for the past two months.

I find it difficult to give them all my attention, for I am bemused at the anachronism of the bows and arrows so casually racked up against the side of the plane as the Amahuaca men help unload the cargo: not three and a half hours have slipped out from under me in my flight to Varadero, but three and a half millennia. The cargo—a drum of kerosene, a precious two dozen of fresh eggs, five kilos of hard candy—is put down helter-skelter in the hut's front room for later sorting, and the mail is exchanged over a rapid lunch. The pilot, fearful of the vagaries of jungle weather, is anxious to return at once.

19

And now for the first time the Amahuaca and I can settle down to stock-taking. For, as I am to discover, this is definitely a mutual affair, a cooperative effort. If my interest is in all things Amahuaca, I am equally a most strange and fascinating creature to them. During the two weeks of this, my first visit in March, and during the five weeks of my second visit in August, Indian-watching and white-watching take on the aspects of a soap opera.

The hut is a palm-thatched, peaked-roofed, two-roomed affair, about eighteen by thirty-six feet over-all. A five-foot split-rail siding forces our Amahuaca audience to go on tiptoe or stand upon a bench to see what is going on. Children peer through the slats; they scamper from one side of the house to the other, whispering loudly about the mysterious goings-on within. I am to have the front room where gear and cargo are spread about, and I find in it half a dozen men sitting on low benches smoking their monkey thighbone pipes, bows and arrows between their legs. Their rumble of talk is punctuated by enormous hawkings and spittings, which are the bane of the ethnologists' tape recordings since a gusty eructation sounds like a mastodon crashing through underbrush. Outside the door the women-folk have spread out woven palm frond mats and have settled down contentedly to a good gossip and a couple of hours of entertainment. The children whoop back and forth between the two groups, to be admonished occasionally in a curiously harsh nasal whine. Forming a more distant yet equally interested circle are the dogs: dogs of all colors and shades, of all degrees of emaciation, of all tones of voice.

There is some confusion at first as Bob Carneiro explains that I will need the room to sleep in (for the Amahuaca have used it as a visiting room), but finally benches and men are moved outside, and I begin unpacking. The door frame is studded with heads, and the chatter increases in volume. Bread: a sigh of delight goes out as we cut up a couple of loaves and pass the slices around. The hard candy gets equal praise. But the *pièce de résistance* is my binocular, which keeps the group outside happily occupied and in fits of laughter as they look through the wrong end while I stow away my gear.

It is a hot day, and the Carneiros suggest a swim. The path slips down past a thorny lime tree and a clump of bamboos, equally thorny, to the high-banked Amahuaquilla—a marvelously cool, clear, and sandy-bottomed rill which runs beneath great trees into the Inuya, a couple of hundred yards and two bends away. I expect some of the Amahuaca to join us. But no, the ethnologists explain, they are very shy, really prudish, about exposing themselves.

I gape, then roar with laughter: how can the Amahuaca men, who go completely naked except for their wide bark belts, be shy about such matters? Yet respectability, it appears, focuses only upon one small area of their anatomy, and for an Amahuaca to lose his belt's protection is as embarrassing for him as for a New Yorker to discover himself bare-bottomed in Times Square. Even when the men wash together in a stream, good manners impel them to turn their backs upon each other. The ladies, for all their unconcealed charms, also behave in the same way, and it was two months before Trudie Dole could persuade a woman to be photographed at her ablutions. Mixed bathing doesn't occur (except between lovers), and any man who comes upon a woman bathing passes discreetly by.

Much refreshed, we slither up the muddy path back to the house. The sun is going down, and a flock of little green parakeets comes shrieking over our heads to roost in a huge tree opposite our hut. As they swirl about in an undisciplined cloud, it appears as if wings and tail are yoked directly to their vocal chords: up go the wings, down goes the tail, and out comes a piercing shriek. Our Amahuaca visitors have returned to their own firesides, and the breeze that funnels up the valley sends the smoke streaming slowly across the airstrip. In the distance I hear the rhythmic pounding of a woman grinding corn. Tunk-a, tunk-a, tunk-a—the notes boom out from the hillside and are echoed flatly back from the slopes behind us. It goes on for two or three minutes, stops as the woman sweeps out the ground corn and pours in another handful of toasted kernels. Hearing the rapid beat, I can imagine myself, fifty, a hundred years ago, thinking it a signal drum.

THE COMMUNITY AT VARADERO is scattered about the juncture of the little Amahuaquilla and the larger Inuya. Varadero is a fairly level plateau which originates at the confluence of the two streams and extends some three hundred and fifty yards into the jungle; it has been totally cleared of trees and underbrush to form the airstrip. This is bordered on one side by a kitchen garden and an occasional citrus tree, while opposite squat a half dozen open-sided palm-thatched huts. At its top end the plateau suddenly humps up into a camel back, while the gully of the Amahuaquilla cuts it off abruptly at the lower end. The six houses along the airstrip form the social and population center of the Varadero settlement, since the remaining huts are scattered within ten or fifteen minutes' walk and are quite hidden in the dense jungle that surrounds the airfield.

The origins of Varadero date back to 1947 when the Peruvian Government, fearful over rumors of an imminent Brazilian invasion, scattered a series of border posts along its eastern frontier. How any military mind could believe that the Brazilians would be able to launch, supply, and transport a task force in this jungle is one mystery. Another is just what it was in this empty countryside that the Brazilians were supposed to attack and conquer. Yet a third mystery involves the function of these border posts: were they really supposed to be able to spot, meet, fight, and rout an enemy? One's mind boggles. But in any case, a couple of platoons were dispatched up the Inuya River to found Puesto Varadero, some hundred and twenty-five miles due west and twenty miles due south of the border.

The border in this area runs through a low, two-thousand-foot plateau which separates the watershed of the Ucayali from those of the three great rivers of western Brazil: the Yuruá, Purús, and Madeira. (See maps in front of book.) A densely forested land, greatly cut up by a maze of streams and short steep hills, it remains to this day the province of eight Panoan Indian tribes and is virtually unexplored by the white man. The tropical forest here is considerably drier than most of the forests watered by the Amazon, and the seventy inches that fall each year make it no wetter than Mobile, Alabama. There is a distinct rainy season, from November through March, when much of this rain comes down in tremendous thunderstorms which burst apocalyptically upon the landscape, though long periods of dreary drizzles may also occur. Apart from the difficulties of moving around, Varadero is a pleasant place; though it gets very hot at midday, its climate is moderated by the twelve-hundred-foot altitude, and by ten o'clock at night one is cool enough to be grateful for a sleeping bag. Then, too, the area is relatively free from noxious insects, it is full of game, and its thick loam soils, covering a limestone and gravel base, are quite productive. Indeed, I can think of far worse places in which to be marooned, which was essentially the fate of the little garrison between 1947 and 1954.

Until 1953 Varadero could only be reached by canoe—a long, tortuous, hundred-and-sixty-mile trip up the Inuya. During its first fifty miles the Inuya looks much like any rain-forest river—brown and slow and sluggish. But soon the river narrows, and for the rest of the journey deep water is interspersed with a myriad of shoals and sandbars over which canoes have to be painfully dragged. All this can change at the burst of a thunderstorm, when the river will rise six feet in as many hours. Then the Inuya becomes a raging torrent, cutting everything down as it carries off the storm's vomit.

To do ten miles a day on the Inuya is doing well, and the garrison had to count at least fourteen days to the nearest supply town, Atalaya, at the confluence of the Tambo and Urubamba rivers. Within a year or two of its establishment, the post had been all but forgotten by the Government, while the men, supplied rarely and skimpily, were forced to live off the jungle, growing their food and hunting in much the same way as the Indians around them.

By 1949 the little garrison had made friendly contact with a few Amahuaca families who lived in the area, and a couple of the women had become camp followers. However, to the Amahuaca, Varadero was merely a place to be visited, for the Indians still retained their traditional diffuse settlement pattern, in which families lived no closer than a half-day's walk from their nearest neighbor. The Amahuaca remained essentially untouched by the garrison at Varadero.

The summer of 1953, however, saw a turning point in Amahuaca history, when two men, Robert L. Russell and Bryan Burtch, arrived at Varadero after a brutal fifteen-day march upriver, during which Russell suffered the exquisite agony of stepping on a sting ray. The two men were members of the Wycliffe

Bible Translators, a missionary group whose training had been specially designed for linguistic work amongst primitive peoples. Behind their sudden appearance at Varadero—the astonishment of the little garrison can well be imagined—lay years of careful planning.

The Wycliffe group was founded some twenty-six years ago by William Cameron Townsend on the proposition that if primitive people were ever fully to appreciate and understand the Bible, it must be available to them in their own language; and, further, that primitive people should be taught to read, and write, in their own language so that they might read the Bible themselves without the intervention and interpretation of others. The consequences of these two simple premises have been remarkable: a worldwide network of linguistic specialists supported by a transportation and communication arm, a medical service, and a commissariat of the utmost ability and resourcefulness.

The group's highly sophisticated linguistic skills are based on the trail-blazing analytical and conceptual approaches of Kenneth L. Pike, one of Townsend's earliest associates. As one of the three major figures who has revolutionized the science of linguistics, he has transmitted his ideas through a continuing series of college courses to young people; they, already imbued with Purpose, could readily understand Townsend's concepts and grasp Pike's methods.

At first the missionary students gathered at the University of Oklahoma for training during summer sessions (hence, Summer Institute of Linguistics, or S. I. L., as the group is generally known in English), though by now Pike's linguistic methodology has spread to a number of other universities. Under Townsend's leadership the linguist-missionaries went out to establish centers from which they could enter into the field, and the Peruvian branch, the Instituto Lingüístico de Verano, was organized some fifteen years ago.

The "Lingüísticos," as the Peruvians call them, were able to convince the Ministry of Education that the most effective way of teaching Spanish to monolingual Indian groups was to develop a bilingual school system, using trained native teachers. Thus, the student would first learn the basic concepts involved in becoming literate in his mother tongue, which could then be transposed easily into the national language.

The S. I. L.'s contract with Peru's Department of Fundamental Education calls for the establishment of their linguists amongst the Montaña Indian tribes with the aim of compiling dictionaries and establishing grammars of the various native tongues, while at the same time devising orthographies that are compatible with Spanish for these languages. This done, the Lingüísticos, in cooperation with the Ministry of Education, train Indian teachers who run Government-supported bilingual schools in the tribes. In this fashion the Government hopes eventually to incorporate into the national culture groups that are presently outside of it. For their part, the Lingüísticos get the necessary fundamentals for translating the Bible into Indian tongues. Their contract with the Government stipulates translations of works of "high moral value," and by adopting Catholic versions of the Bible, they have avoided collisions over dogma.

Actually Russell and Burtch were the second Lingüístico mission to the Amahuaca. The first, under Dale W. Kietzman, began the work of language analysis with an acculturated group located near the mouth of the Sepahua River, a logical choice since these particular Amahuaca were bilingual. Kietzman, however, could not continue because of sickness (and also, it has been reported locally, because this Amahuaca group were irrepressible thieves, which made his life extremely difficult). And so it was that Russell and Burtch, armed with one hundred and fifty words of Amahuaca and what few linguistic notes Kietzman had been able to make, arrived at Varadero, only to find that the nearest group of Amahuaca were yet another day's walk away. Early the following evening, after shivering through the jungle from Varadero in a cold, windy rain, Russell and Burtch

> …arrived at the clearing of Nisho, high up on a hilltop, and found a group of men seated on low balsa-wood benches around a small fire, bow and arrows in hand. The bodies of the men were painted red-orange with *achiote*.

Russell goes on to write:

> The people were not too much impressed by us, and, with the exception of Nisho, they remained seated on their benches…. Two soldiers had taken Bryan and me to this Amahuaca clearing. We probably would not have been able to find it without their help…. In all, it was a friendly visit. I remember that the Amahuaca men passed around a small clay bowl that had some sort of yellow liquid in it, and we all one by one partook of this. I later found out that this was *xuqui ayati* [the Amahuaca maize soup]…. In addition, a pipe with very strong-smelling tobacco made its way around the circle. Bryan and I did not participate in the smoking, and fortunately the host did not seem to be offended at all. At least he didn't say anything. As a matter of fact, no one said much of anything that late afternoon and evening…. At this point we didn't know what to think about the Amahuaca. They are not too expressive about anything—they didn't say much, didn't smile, didn't show much emotion of any kind.

"But at least," Russell concludes, "they were hospitable." The host's wife gave the two missionaries food, and they, in turn, shared what they had with the Amahuaca, giving them "a few trinkets such as needles, thread, and mentholated vaseline. These," Russell adds, "were readily accepted and, I assume, appreciated, although there was still not much display of emotions."

Russell later commented on this:

> At first we didn't know what to think about the Amahuaca and their emotional numbness. Now that we know them better, we have come to the conclusion that on special occasions those who are behaving in proper Amahuaca fashion hide their emotions. The meeting of strangers is one of these special occasions. Furthermore, it seems that to conceal the emotions and appear to be uninterested is a highly accepted mode of behavior for almost any social occasion. Underneath, the Amahuaca are a friendly, inquisitive people.

The following day an Amahuaca who knew a little Spanish agreed to teach the Americans Amahuaca and to interpret for them. Through him they arranged for some Indians to return to the Inuya River with them to help them make a clearing and build a house.

Russell and Burtch's decision to settle down near the army garrison, rather than amongst any particular family of Amahuaca, was based on a number of considerations: since there were no Amahuaca at Varadero, it would avoid the dangers of "playing favorites"; it would reinforce the attractions of the existing military settlement; it would allay any suspicions that the garrison might have of foreigners; and, finally, the outpost might be of assistance in case of emergency. The first summer they were at Varadero the two Lingüísticos managed to clear a jungle patch, plant their *chacra* (vegetable garden), and throw up a temporary shelter. In this they were helped by two Amahuaca men, one of whom eventually became the first Amahuaca to settle in Varadero. Indeed, the help given the missionaries was crucial, for it would have been impossible for them to have stayed the whole of the summer: the Lingüísticos had run out of food.

Associations with the little garrison were friendly: the soldiers were delighted to see someone from the "outside"; while the missionaries, in turn, were pleased by the fact that the Amahuaca did, indeed, come to visit the post. Good relations were cemented when Russell, with great effort, extended the open ground near the garrison into a very short airstrip so that the soldiers were able to fly in sorely needed supplies via the Lingüístico's plane. Their appreciation was shown by celebrating the Fourth of July in the Americans' honor—at four in the morning! Sneaking up to their hut unannounced, the Peruvians let off a tremendous fusillade, loud enough to waken the dead and scary enough for Russell to believe that a major Indian raid was in progress.

These, then, are the origins of Varadero—or more exactly, Puesto Varadero. For the Amahuaca village that exists today—seventeen families strong— contains the largest single collection of Amahuaca known in the Montaña. This village is the direct result of Russell's efforts (a year after the two men arrived, malaria forced Burtch to drop out), and not of the military garrison. It is the result of patient, laborious, even agonizing work; it is the product of one man's vision supported and sustained by the collective skills of the organization behind him.

EVERYTHING I SEE ABOUT ME as I sit down to dinner is a testament to Russell's efforts: the house that was so cheerfully loaned us; the kerosene refrigerator; the power plant that runs the radio and pumps the water and sharpens the tools; the pressure stove and beds and mosquito netting. This jungle hut, with the petty comforts accumulated over the past decade, is a practical, as well as symbolic, outpost of Western civilization.

The anachronisms and the contrasts are all about us in the strange mélange of the known and the fanciful: a kerosene lamp that lights up stainless steel cutlery, plastic glasses and plates laid out on a plastic tablecloth. But the plates are filled with howler-monkey stew covering a bed of rice and beans seasoned with a blink of *ají,* a fiendish little red pepper. And the sheets that screen kitchen from sleeping quarters are crawling with a mass of insects, most of which I have seen only in museum collections: a rhinoceros beetle; a curious fulgorid, whose hollow snout makes it look like a miniature alligator; a cicada, with enormous eyes and the dismaying habit of squealing loudly and plaintively whenever phototropism impels the wretch to an auto-da-fé upon the lamp.

I crawl under my mosquito net and onto my sleeping bag (it is still hot enough two hours after sundown to appreciate the light breeze), and the Carneiros are listening to the BBC short wave: "Paris . . . the Prime Minister . . . Association Football. . . ." It all seems infinitely far away. Through the wall staves I can dimly make out the fires glimmering in the huts across the airstrip. Amahuaca voices sputter and flicker like the flames—now loud, now soft, finally steadying to a mumble occasionally rent by a snort of laughter.

It must be midnight when I wake up with a start. I lie there tensely listening to the night sounds—the penetrating, all-encompassing whine of katydids, the distant rumble of a troop of night monkeys, the scurrying insects busy about my room, the rifle shot of an exploding bamboo—but they all seem identifiable, and I relax and crawl into my sleeping bag for it is by now quite cold. All of a sudden I freeze again: "Ork, ork, ork . . . orrkkk." The rapid croaking slows down gradually and is finally choked off in a most grisly way. I spend an unhappy ten minutes imagining what is being done to whom, when once again the murderer gets busy on another victim: "Ork, orrk . . . orrkk." It is only in the morning that I discover that the sounds are produced by a small, serenading rodent.

The quietest time of the day is just before sunrise, when the night animals have gone off to sleep and the day shift has yet to come on. This morning Varadero is transformed into a different world: It is submerged in fog, a dense, murky mist, under which the heavy dew turns the airstrip into a sheet of polished pewter. Swelling and swirling mysteriously, it pours in one vast, soundless cataract, off the plateau and into the river gully below. Then suddenly, with the improbable rapidity of a stage set lighted by an amateur, the sun comes up, and the fog, glistening now like pink cotton candy, vanishes in bits and pieces as if a giant mouth were gulping it down, leaving the air a milky blue. A late owl flits by silently. In the tall tree shading the huts across the airstrip, the green parakeets come to life and, like a swarm of ill-tempered commuters, go winging their way across the valley and over the hills.

Breakfast is a cheerful affair. The precious eggs are scrambled, and the last loaf sliced for toast. Three men appear as we finish our coffee. Lounging against the door frame, they talk to Trudie Dole.

"They say that Maxoopo and Jawachiwayamba floated the canoe yesterday," Trudie reports. "Let's go look at it."

A canoe? This is interesting news, for the Varadero Amahuaca, as far as can be determined, have not made one within living memory. This one has been the idea and almost the sole work of Jawachiwayamba, who got to know about such matters when he worked lumber downstream. Now the morning's plans are revised, for the canoe is half an hour's journey up the Inuya.

As we start along the path, we are joined by Pansitimba, a lad of about twelve. He is a quiet boy, handsome in a rather flat-featured way, and his deeply slanted eyes have a slight cast to them. He has a tip-tilted nose with a scar on the end of it—the result of a vampire-bat bite a few years back. Well built and tall for his age, the parasite-distended stomach of the younger child has nearly left him.

My inadequacies as a city dweller are immediately manifest when the trail drops about thirty feet to the Inuya in a series of mud slicks. While the Indians skip their way down as though they were on stairs, arriving in the river without even a splash, I have to skid down on my bottom, ignominiously clutching the nearest available root or vine or helping hand—a performance that brings on some good-natured bantering from the Amahuaca.

It is an utterly delicious morning as we set off upstream, the knee-deep water marvelously cool and clear as it runs over a sandy bed. At seven-thirty it is still chilly enough for us to welcome the sun whenever the banks widen sufficiently to let it in, and its rays start up a dazzle of diamonds as the heavy dew on the leaves catches the light. The Amahuaca are ahead, keeping a sharp lookout for fish, their bows at the ready. At the first bend, where a sandstone cliff about thirty feet high forms a deep ESS in the river, the men freeze, and their long arrows, like pointers' tails, indicate a school. But these fish are too wary (for this is the women's bathing area), and the men go on, desultorily poking into all likely holes on the off chance that something—agouti, bird, or catfish—might be in possession.

Scrambling over a fallen tree trunk, I am engulfed by an efflorescence of—cinnamon?—allspice? Pansitimba, who has quietly dropped back to dog my bumbling progress and so enjoy the mystery of my binoculars, scampers up the bank with his bow at arm's length and manages to snag an invisibly small white bloom off a twenty-foot bush. "Is it good for anything? How is it used?" Pansitimba doesn't know, so the men are called back from their fruitless stalk. The plant, however, only smells; it is not good for anything; and besides, stinging ants live on it.

The canoe, when we finally come upon it, is a disappointment; twenty-odd feet long, it has a width of some eighteen inches and is crudely carved from a bright, reddish wood. One of our guides, who turns out to be a great ham, hops onto the stern, standing tall and straight, arms crossed around his bow and arrows until his picture is taken. But though a loud-mouthed extrovert, he at least has style, which is more than can be said for either of his two companions: one has club feet; the other seems burdened with the problems of a young father: his wife recently presented him with twins. The ill-hewn canoe holds little interest for me, and I wander up the Inuya with Pansitimba, still firmly glued to the binoculars.

PANSITIMBA amused me all morning with his half-man, half-boy complexities: at one moment he was the serious adult solemnly stalking a nervous fish; at the next he was all boy, using both hands to throw a stone so that it hummed loudly through the air, or getting a piggyback ride amidst squeals of laughter.

Amahuaca children have few true games: most of their play imitates adult occupations. Like his American counterpart with a .22, the young Amahuaca boy is forever letting fly with bow and arrow at the targets natural to his age and capacity. Thus, one of Pansitimba's brothers, a most wretched brat, can be found stalking game appropriate to his six years—a rhinoceros beetle, a toad, or a lizard, perhaps even a hapless sleeping dog—with a tiny bow made of a bent twig and arrows cut from the midrib of a palm frond. As he crawls on knees and elbows, he presents a most comical sight: his little bow at full draw weaves back and forth in the opposite direction to the wiggle of his naked, dusty bottom; he has his tongue firmly clenched between his teeth and a look of utter concentration on his pudgy face. Older boys may let fly at a papaya, a hummingbird's nest, hopefully at a fish. But Pansitimba, as a serious hunter approaching manhood, is beyond such unproductive target practice, more from fear of damaging his arrows than because he might lose them. Indeed, lost arrows are amazingly infrequent, particularly when one considers the vegetation into which they can disappear.

One day when I had gone up the Amahuaquilla with Pansitimba and three men, we chanced upon the nest of a toucan. One of the birds was standing watch on a branch, some sixty feet up. Each man had four arrows with him, and they loosed every one of them—without any effect except to get the toucan to look down his supercilious yellow beak at the noisy crew below.

Pansitimba's uncle fletching an arrow; Pansitimba and family at breakfast before the hunt; father and son straighten arrows with glowing coals. Hunter with Harpy eagle; the famous dugout canoe; a boa constrictor. The trip home by water.

The virgin jungle here consists of three layers. The middle section includes small palms, thorny bamboo, and a variegated mess of softwoods, all growing thirty to fifty feet high. Above this, the vast silk cotton trees, extending one hundred to one hundred and fifty feet, loom to form an uneven second story. Below these two layers is a dense underbrush: ferns, stinging nettles, seedlings, and an enormous variety of bushes varying in height between mid-thigh and mid-chest. Certainly a miserable place from which to recover arrows. Imagine my astonishment when Pansitimba, told to fetch them, was back in ten minutes with all twelve.

Any bowman in the jungle learns to take a sight along the flight of an arrow he has loosed, so that by walking along this line, he can recover it. Where to a city dweller one part of the jungle looks very much like any other, to an Amahuaca each is recognizably different. When a hunter is in hot pursuit of game, he will rarely stop to recover an arrow, leaving this to his return trip or even to another day.

A child's first arrows are not even fletched, but a full scale arrow requires a lot of work: a man can turn out four (the usual number carried on a hunting trip) in a couple of hours if he is not interrupted and if the materials are all at hand. Pansitimba's father, an excellent hunter, is the best bow and arrow maker of the group at Varadero. He, like all the other men, has a cache of materials carefully put up in the eaves of his house: a stack of arrow cane used for the shaft, length of dried bamboo for arrowheads, slats of *pijuayo* palm from which he whittles shanks for joining arrowhead to shaft, and, in the neat oblong reed basket, beeswax, cotton thread, and resin. Here, too, carefully wrapped up, is a precious collection of feathers, some used for decoration and some for fletching. The latter most often come from the wings of the *paujil*, the largest of game birds of the area, a fowl drably dressed in black mourning with a fleshy red-orange growth over its beak. Pansitimba, like any Amahuaca male, can identify the maker of a particular arrow by the way the feathers are cut, or by the way the bamboo blade is shaped or decorated, or in the way in which the various parts of the arrow are tied together.

A boy's first hunting grounds are the stream beds, for the waterways offer him an easy draw, a quiet stalk, and dense cover amidst the bushes that line the banks. While the birds and beasts that inhabit its narrow reaches tend to be as small in scale as the little hunter (the bigger game has been driven into the denser forest areas by the adults), he rarely comes back empty-handed: a small fish or two, freshwater mussels, crabs and crayfish are almost certainties; the watercourse, as an aerial flyway for a whole raft of small birds, offers access to nests that can be robbed of eggs and young; even an incautious rodent can be found, on occasion, sleeping off its nocturnal depredations in a burrow in the riverbank. A species of utterly silent gray sand martins is probably too fast for the young hunter, as are the kingfisher, a dim flycatcher, and a fluttery, cheerful little finch, whose red cap contrasts handsomely with black back and white belly. Almost certainly out of range of the boy's bow are the crews of raucous macaws, much prized for their decorative red and blue feathers, which return at sunset in a welter of pirate oaths to roost in the tall trees along the river bed.

37

Nonetheless, many inaccessible animals can be caught in another way. For Pansitimba, like any Amahuaca, is an excellent mimic of bird and animal calls, and a good mimic will keep many a timid animal interested long enough for the hunter to creep into bow range. In some cases a hunter will even get the animal to come to him by sounding a mating cry; any number of male spider monkeys have fallen to an Amahuaca imitating a female calling to her mate.

Stone throwing and climbing are two other children's games that turn out to be valuable hunting skills. Stones are used to flush animals out of hiding, while the hunter who knows how to climb trees can go after game that stays in the forest canopy and is invisible from the ground. Maxoopo, the owner of the canoe, killed three howler monkeys by climbing up a liana to the branch of a tree which overlooked the chattering band. Getting at the honey of a stingless little black bee involves not merely a scramble with a climbing loop, but much work with a machete to reach the dark, acrid combs secreted inside the hollow bole. The hunter gulps handfuls of the honey while hanging casually a hundred feet in the air, but his delight is short-lived when he becomes covered inches deep in a buzzing, crawling, tickling mass of tiny insects, whose only defense is to smother the invader. The latter is finally driven to find refuge in the nearest stream, there to wash off his patina of bees and honey.

No father instructs his son directly, and a boy learns hunting skills by both doing and observing. Amahuaca men hunt every second or third day, and Pansitimba's father and uncle often leave on a hunt together, though they frequently part company along the way. The boy is usually asked to come along, for one of a father's delights is having his son accompany him. If Pansitimba decides to go with them (and the choice is usually his, although his father is disappointed should he refuse), he is expected to do his share of the work, beating bushes, keeping an eye cocked for animals, participating in the kill, and shooting fish along the way.

With his bow and arrows an Amahuaca is armed equally for bird or beast or fish, and wherever he goes, his eye is attuned to the forest around him. Beehive or bird's nest or fruit tree, sooner or later they will all trigger a spate of activity, since foraging supplies the delicacies that round out the staple diet of fish, monkey, peccary, tapir, deer, fowl, manioc, and maize. There is very little that the Amahuaca refuse to eat, since, unlike most of the other Montaña tribes, they have but few totem animals that may not be killed (and most of these prohibitions are obeyed more in the breach than the observance).

Pansitimba acquires his hunting lore, not by being told, "See this tree? Its fruit attracts *paujil*," but indirectly, usually when his father is eating a meal in company with other men. Here talk centers on their major occupation, and preoccupation—hunting, and in vast detail. A recent tapir chase will find the men discussing how fresh were its footprints, its droppings; how the hunter had followed the spoor and where it led; where he had made his ambush, how he had built his blind, whether he had used as bait the same kind of fruit that the animal had been eating (determined by examining the feces for seeds); and on and on.

MAXOOPO'S TWO HOUSEHOLDS are halfway up the hill on the other side of the Inuya from the airstrip. The trail is quite steep in spots and, when wet, extremely slippery. What takes me twenty-five breathless and unpleasant minutes this morning, takes an Amahuaca no more than ten. Nevertheless, I sympathize with Maxoopo's wives, who carry water up twice a day.

Most Amahuaca build their houses quite some distance from streams for fear of attack, and before Varadero became a settled community, trails were carefully hidden and usually booby-trapped with large thorns from the spiny bamboo. These thorns, as I found to my cost, are extraordinarily tough, easily penetrating the double-thick sole of my basketball sneakers. What they would do to the bare foot of any unwary walker, I shudder to think; sowing a defensive minefield of these thorns must have discouraged many a raiding party.

As I pant, slip, and scramble up the trail, I hear the drum roll of a woman grinding maize, the hollow notes barely muffled by the towering trees of the virgin jungle. Though it is ten in the morning, it is still cool under the dense canopy a hundred feet overhead; the path winds madly, avoiding here a stand of stinging nettles, there a buttress root, or crossing a gully on the trunk of a fallen giant.

Maxoopo has cleared about half an acre on a level spot about two thirds of the way up the hill. Two big open-sided huts, end to end, house his wives, while the two smaller shelters flanking them are occupied by his married son and by the mother of his second wife. Around the houses the hard-packed earth is littered with old bones, potsherds, corncobs. Yesterday's mess has yet to be cleaned up. A mangy bitch gnaws on a fish head while a tame green parrot flitters about the huts.

Wando, the mother-in-law, came to visit her daughter a month ago, at which time Maxoopo built her this temporary shelter. She is a spritely old girl, dressed in bits and pieces of Western clothing, nearly toothless, and somewhat embarrassed over her recently cropped gray hair (it makes her look like Gertrude Stein). The Amahuaca, despite their extreme personal cleanliness, are occasionally afflicted by head lice, and then the only salvation from the intolerable itching is to hack off the hair so as to simplify the job of hunting down the parasites.

Wando is sitting straight-legged in front of her hut, rapidly rolling out a two-foot length of clay, which she pinches onto the end of a previous coil. Once in a while, as her deft fingers squeeze the long thin sausage into place, she finds a piece of gravel which has to be excised.

"Daughter's clay isn't very good, Younger Sister," she remarks to Trudie Dole, who has sat down to sketch the process. (Wando, like all Amahuaca—and like many other primitive people—goes to elaborate lengths to avoid naming anyone, for fear of bringing them to the attention of evil spirits.) "Too many of her pots are breaking while they are being fired. She will have to find another clay pit which has less stones." The ethnologist and the old lady are good friends, and they chatter away as the pot is finished.

39

Setting it out to dry beside the three others she has made this morning, Wando asks, "You wouldn't have an empty can—a big one—would you?" Alas, the ethnologists don't have such a prized commodity, but Trudie promises to save her the next one they open.

Wando's daughter, Rohanhno, sits nearby at her mortar. An open-faced woman in her late thirties, she is Maxoopo's second and favorite wife. Four of her children are alive today: three boys by Maxoopo and a daughter by a previous marriage. For a while this girl shared Maxoopo's favors with her mother before eloping downstream with a homeward-bound soldier from the garrison. Another daughter of Rohanhno's first marriage is dead. She had become the second wife of one of Maxoopo's brothers, but was killed—poisoned out of jealousy by her co-wife. The only child now living with Rohanhno is her youngest boy, a three-year-old who is teasing the dogs and scrambling all over her as she grinds her maize.

Rohanhno's mortar is made from a four-foot length of hardwood, cut from a tree bole, split in half and hollowed out to make an open-ended trough. Her pestle, a massive, ax-shaped slab, is rocked on its beam ends over the toasted maize kernels which she pours in, a handful at a time. By now she has ground over a gallon of the coarse meal called *muto,* and goes to her hut to turn it into a soup.

The hut is about forty feet long by about twenty wide and rises to about twelve feet at the ridge pole. The sharply peaked thatched roof comes to within some three feet of the ground but otherwise is utterly without walls or partitions. The one large room is neatly arranged; the floor has been recently swept clear of the usual detritus of banana peels, corncobs, animal bones, and old ashes.

At one end the star-shaped cooking fire is smoldering around a large clay pot of boiling water for the *muto* that Rohanhno has just ground. At the other end two sticks are stuck into the ground about three feet apart; they are vertical elements from which Rohanhno's loom dangles, for she is making herself a new skirt. Racked neatly in the thatching are Maxoopo's second bow and a bundle of arrows, together with his reed box of prized possessions. Also in the thatching, at about shoulder height, are a couple of platforms: a combination fruit and vegetable larder and place for storing pots, bits of cloth, leftover yarn and string, and a large tin can vastly precious because it has a tight lid. Hammocks, now neatly hanging from one of the timbers of the main frame, are slung around the night fire which is kept going to take the chill out of the air; often the whole family may pile into a hammock, head to foot on the diagonal.

Climbing is an important hunting skill; an Amahuaca with bow and arrows is armed for bird, beast, or fish. Pansitimba helps build a hut: first the frame, then the thatching. But a man's major occupation is still hunting.

The maize that Rohanhno has been grinding forms one of the major staples of Amahuaca life. Toasted and ground into *muto,* it may be eaten immediately and has a faint but pleasant flavor of peanuts. It is also possessed of an intense, almost piercing dryness, rather like, I imagine, the biscuit the Red Queen offered poor Alice to assuage her thirst. The Amahuaca are forever munching handfuls of it (which probably explains their high rate of dental decay, as the starch remains in the mouth long enough to ferment): the men carry some *muto* when they go hunting; the women when they go to work in their *chacras.* There is always a potful around the house, and visitors are automatically offered some when they arrive. In addition to the hot soup, *muto* is also the base for a cool, lightly fermented drink. Made by chewing a few mouthfuls of *muto* and spitting it into a pot of maize gruel, the thick soup is then left to stand for a few days, to become a "near beer."

According to the ethnologists' calculations, a two-person family at Varadero consumes around one hundred and seventy-five ears of maize every six days. At a quarter of a pound of kernels per ear, this represents a daily consumption of some three pounds of carbohydrates per capita. But it is by no means all starch. Because the Amahuaca do not remove the germ from the kernel, most of the high protein content and valuable oils of maize are retained. While not all of this maize is eaten—a lot is turned into the "near beer" or fed to the dogs—an astonishing amount is, and a woman must count on spending at least an hour a day at her mortar.

Maxoopo has a granary located on a steep hill behind his huts, just above his *chacra.* It looks much like any other Amahuaca hut, sitting foursquare on the hill crest, though perhaps a bit shorter than the usual dwelling. Inside, a loft, about three feet off the ground, runs for half the granary's length and half of this platform is tightly packed with last year's maize crop—about twenty-five thousand ears, the ethnologists estimate, a clear indication of the role that maize plays in the Amahuaca diet.

THE TRAIL THAT LEADS TO THE GRANARY climbs almost vertically in a last desperate spurt to the crest of the hill, where we are rewarded with a delicious breeze and an incomparable view. For the hillside falls away so steeply that we seem to be walking along the top of the forest: an ocean of green rolls away to the horizon. Here and there great rashes of purple or red or yellow catch the eye: vast patches of flowering vines as brilliant as any butterfly—sargassos on the billowing jungle canopy. Alfred R. Wallace, who explored the Amazon Basin over a hundred years ago, remarked on the difficulties of a botanist in a jungle, where "many of these trees . . . [have not a] single blossom . . . at less height than a hundred feet. . . . It is only on the outside of the great domes of verdure . . . that flowers are produced. . . ." And then, in a charming,

47

almost Verneian fantasy, he wistfully suggests that "the whole glory of these forests [can] only be seen by sailing gently in a balloon over the undulating flowery surface ... such a treat is perhaps reserved for the traveller of a future age."

The face of the hill had been cleared for *chacras*, but I would have passed through Maxoopo's garden quite unknowingly, for the plants were growing amidst a tangled mass of chest-high brush. This was the second year that one of Maxoopo's wives had planted this clearing, and already the vanguard of the invading forest was growing madly around, over, even on the crumbling debris of tree trunks, a barely visible reminder of the virgin forest that Maxoopo had cut down just twelve months before.

Actually Maxoopo has two *chacras:* this one at Varadero, and another some distance away. For like many slash-and-burn agriculturalists, the Amahuaca can be considered seminomadic in that they will rotate concurrently through two *chacras* which are often quite far apart. A new clearing just hacked out of the jungle produces the major yield, and its surplus is carried over to the following year for seed and food. The second year's crop from this original patch is so greatly reduced by the invading scrub that it will not carry the family through the season; thus the family must ready another clearing during this period. By the third year the original patch can only be gleaned for sports that have somehow managed to survive here and there.

In this sense Varadero is a part-time community, as the families are absent three and four months during the year when they go to live near their other *chacras*, two, three, sometimes even five days' walk away. Eventually, of course, all of the good arable land at Varadero will have been cut over, and then the settlement will have to move to another district. For it is vastly unprofitable, in terms of the labor required, to cut a *chacra* from a once-cleared area if virgin forest is available. The large trees of the primary forest, which so effectively reduce the density of the scrub growth beneath them, take a long time to grow, and most Indians consider that a man will not be able to clear the same spot twice in a lifetime.

An area adjacent to Maxoopo's second-year *chacra* has been newly cleared, and here man's technique of slash-and-burn agriculture is all too evident. Over the blasted earth a vast collection of trees lie scattered as in a gigantic game of spillikins; their trunks are carbonized by the fire that was set to clear the underbrush. Every step raises a cloud of charcoal in this dismal, almost lunar landscape. But already the seeds planted but a few weeks previously are sprouting, the pale yellow-green shoots scattered about four feet apart amongst the fallen logs and through the thick, greasy ashes.

Pansitimba with his dog early one morning; later with his uncle, he uses a bamboo-stem "bucket" to quench smoldering trunks near the huts; boys throwing stones, another valued hunting skill.

Slash-and-burn agriculture: each Amahuaca clears five to ten acres of jungle a year; one major crop is produced before the invading jungle overwhelms it. Even the enormous kapok tree is felled.

48

Sugar cane, sweet potatoes and squash, peanuts, maize, cotton, watermelon, and gourds grow in the family *chacra*. And immediately below the granary, on the far side of the hill is another clearing. Maxoopo himself planted some of this crop, for there are luxurious stands of tobacco and arrow cane for his own needs. These merge into still another household plot of rather dull shrubs with dark green, deeply indented leaves and a knobbly stem running up to head height: manioc, the second basic staple of the Montaña Indians. Manioc, yuca, cassava—the words bring back a rush of childhood memories of pirates and castaways and South Sea Islanders; of offensive English puddings which looked as if they were made (as I recall chanting dismally with my table mates) of "frogs' eggs, frogs' eggs" or "fish-eyes, fisheyes," depending upon the size of the tapioca.

There is even a lime tree near one of the huts, for the Amahuaca have a keen appreciation of the exotic plant and are forever begging seeds of new varieties. Thus when I brought some oranges to Varadero, the women carefully saved their pips for later planting. However, the Amahuaca make little, if any, attempt to cultivate the wild fruits that are scattered sparsely through the jungle. These are usually eaten on the spot, though sometimes they may be brought back. Rohanhno came to us one day with a small basket of dark red fruit which tasted remarkably like cherries. How shocked I was to hear that she had felled the tree in order to pick them. But when I remembered that there are at least twenty square miles for every man, woman, and child in the Varadero "territory," I realize the meaninglessness of my dismay at such destruction. As she put it succinctly: "Older Brother, there are many more such trees. All I have to do if I want more fruit is to go and find them."

If only the women could just "go and find" their staples. For most of the work in the *chacras* is done by women. Although men clear off the forest and plant the manioc (and may even help with bananas, papayas and sugar cane) the women and girls do all the rest: from carrying out the roots and seed to the *chacra* and planting them deep, to picking the crop and carrying it back to house and granary. When one adds to this that women have to bring in firewood, fetch water, grind maize, collect clay, and make pots and do all of the other household chores—the spinning and weaving, the cooking and cleaning—one begins to appreciate how burdensome is the purely physical aspect of their lives. Moreover, they have to do all this while rearing children. It is no wonder that a woman faced with the brutal labor of carrying a seventy-pound load of maize or wood or manioc, plus a toddler in a sling, plus another barely able to walk, takes so readily to infanticide.

MAXOOPO, who has the distinction of being the owner of the first canoe in Varadero's history, has had problems with Pacho, his wayward daughter. Curiously, canoe and daughter were part of the same problem. About ten years ago, when Pacho was about a year old, Maxoopo had agreed with his brother-in-law, who lived on the Curiuja River, to marry their respective daughters to each other's sons. But while Maxoopo's eldest boy later did marry his predetermined wife, Pacho refused to go along with the arrangement. And this is where the canoe came in. For the maker of the canoe, Jawachiwayamba, began to court Pacho, and she was obviously interested in him. Jawachiwayamba is a large, stocky, heavily muscled man in his late thirties, with an adventurous disposition. He is a recent arrival at Varadero, having had a *chacra* a few days' walk downstream. There he had been married to a woman of about his own age, a widow with two teen-aged sons, and had remained with her until their own two daughters had suddenly died. At this time he left his wife to work for a lumber *patrón* near the mouth of the Inuya. He was gone quite some time—so long, in fact, that his wife became convinced that he had died, and decided to move upriver to Varadero with the two sons from her first marriage. Here she eventually settled down with a young man some fifteen years her junior, barely older than her eldest boy.

Jawachiwayamba, however, was by no means dead. He eventually turned up in Varadero, and when he found his wife remarried, he was properly indignant. But there was little he could do about it, short of murdering the new husband—which was really not to be considered: not only were the two men cousins, but Jawachiwayamba would in all likelihood have been killed in return, as the younger man was related to quite a number of the families then living at Varadero. All Jawachiwayamba could do, then, was to grumble while leading the uncomfortable life of a bachelor and keep a sharp lookout for a possible mate.

Jawachiwayamba's prospects, however, appeared dim indeed. The only girl of marriageable age at Varadero was Pacho, who not only was spoken for, but she and Jawachiwayamba were not in the preferred kinship relationship to marry. In addition, Maxoopo was hoping that his daughter's marriage to her Curiuja cousin would strengthen the bonds between the two families, bonds that had become weaker since his sister's recent death.

But Maxoopo did not take into account Jawachiwayamba's influence on Pacho. Jawachiwayamba, as a man in his prime, a fine hunter, a traveler to far places, and clearly an excellent provider, must have appeared a far more glamorous and desirable mate to Pacho than her cousin, who was a callow boy in his early teens, the baby fat still visible.

Cuho, Pansitimba's aunt, in a rare moment of relaxation—children are not far away and have to be looked after, whether a woman is planting or carrying back the crop, keeping house, cleaning game, carrying water, making a pot, roasting maize, or weaving.

Pacho may have been eleven when I first saw her: a rather sullen, pubescent girl much interested in the frivolities of life. Perhaps she realized all too clearly the lifetime of backbreaking labor that was to be her lot. For every once in a while she would come out of her gloom to show a twinkling, flirtatious disposition, becoming, almost desperately, a playful young girl. It became clear that Pacho was in no mood to become a *hausfrau* when a few months previously she was abducted by Coyaso, Jawachiwayamba's unmarried stepson. While she did not protest too much at first, what with the excitement of it all, she was back within a few days, complaining bitterly of the work and that Coyaso was both lazy and a bad hunter.

While Pacho's abduction had been undertaken with her mother's consent, her father's position was somewhat ambivalent, since he was still publicly holding to his original commitment. Indeed, when she returned, Maxoopo firmly announced to all and sundry that Pacho was indeed going to marry her betrothed. Thus all seemed settled when Pacho's cousin appeared to claim her, and a large group from Varadero suddenly formed to accompany the young couple part of their journey back. There was Maxoopo, his two wives and seven assorted children; an elderly couple who wanted to visit some of their friends along the trail; and, curiously, Jawachiwayamba, on the excuse that he was paying a call upon a relative: he claimed he was going along to visit Maxoopo's father. But two days later the entire Varadero group was back, Pacho included, her little face black as a thundercloud. She had balked at going any farther than her grandfather's.

Jawachiwayamba's decision to make a play for Pacho can be traced to this event. He then began to spend most of his time up at Maxoopo's, helping with the usual chores. Not so usual was Jawachiwayamba's work on the canoe, which he began at this time. It was clearly a formal bid, with Jawachiwayamba viewing the canoe as bride service for Pacho, while the girl, by her actions and gestures, was making it clear that she now considered herself his wife: they would go visiting as a couple, disappear into the bushes to make love, wash and play in the stream.

However, her cousin on the Curiuja had not given up. One month after his abortive attempt to collect Pacho, he and some dozen kinsfolk arrived late one afternoon at Varadero. It was quite an occasion down at the airstrip, but it was only when Maxoopo's wives finally left to prepare their dinner that the visitors could start asking the important questions: "Where is Pacho?" "Why isn't she here?" "What is she doing?" Their Varadero hosts were careful not to tell about Pacho's recent behavior. As for Maxoopo, while he still felt that his nephew was the proper claimant, he must nevertheless have had qualms about not having discouraged Jawachiwayamba's suit. Certainly he acted guiltily. For while his Curiuja relatives and their Varadero hosts were enjoying an evening of chanting and "near beer," he packed up his two wives, their children, and his mother-in-law and slipped away to his downstream hut, leaving Pacho to fend for herself.

Jawachiwayamba, too, must have felt that his rights were not secure enough to challenge the Curiuja cousin's title, since he tamely went to the party for the visitors at the airstrip. Pacho, for her part, cried bitterly, wailing that she would not leave, that she would run away before they could take her. The next morning the Curiuja group set off, accompanied by a sullen, sniffling Pacho and Coyaso. It was only after they had left that Jawachiwayamba began to voice his grievances, enumerating all the work he had done for Maxoopo. But he did so more as a man resigned than wronged; he seemed to acknowledge the cousin's rights.

It took only a day this time for Pacho to return. And now it became clear that this was what Jawachiwayamba had been awaiting: if the cousin wasn't man enough to keep the girl—and the youth had already failed twice—certainly he, Jawachiwayamba, was. And with that, he took Pacho off to the Purús. It was a strong claim indeed, now that Jawachiwayamba had made up his mind. For he is a formidable man—tough, cunning, resourceful—someone to be feared if it ever came to a showdown. The cousin was hopelessly outclassed and knew it. Now he could only hope to carry off Pacho in a raid, and for this he would need the help of adult relatives. To date there has been no such attempt, and it seems unlikely that there will ever be one. Jawachiwayamba has finally got his wife, and Maxoopo his canoe.

Naturally there was much talk at Varadero about these stirring events. The largest group, while disapproving somewhat of Jawachiwayamba as Pacho's husband (after all, the two were in an undesirable kinship relationship), accepted the union with little discussion. A small minority, however, led by Coyaso, claimed that Pacho was bad: she shouldn't have left her cousin since she had already been paid for (a reference to the recent marriage between her brother and the cousin's sister); and they would disown her. As for Jawachiwayamba's having made the canoe for Maxoopo, that they discounted. Proper bride service, said the clique, would be to assist Maxoopo in clearing a *chacra*, building a hut, giving him a mortar and pestle. Since Jawachiwayamba had produced none of these, obviously bride service had not been rendered.

It was a curious group, for both stepsons had been very friendly with Jawachiwayamba. Perhaps the sudden cooling came from the fact that Jawachiwayamba had not paid "wife balm" to Coyaso, who, as a bachelor standing in the proper kinship relationship to Pacho, was entitled to a token payment from any successful suitor. It was an odd display of temper: giving bride service (outside of two families exchanging daughters in marriage) is not frequent these days amongst the Amahuaca and is certainly not exacted as heavily as Coyaso intimated; and wife balm, too, is more notable for its absence than for its payment. However, Coyaso claimed that had he been successful in his original attempt to abduct Pacho, he would have indemnified the cousin with a bundle of arrows; while had Pacho remained with the cousin, the latter would have cleared a small *chacra* for Coyaso. In any event it should be noted that Coyaso is indeed a lazy young man, as Pacho claimed, and that at this time his *chacra* was overgrown with weeds.

THE COURSE OF MOST MARRIAGES is usually smoother: the couple merely go off and live together. Courtship as such does not occur, for while a man will spend much time at the girl's home, his outward attention is not directed so much to her as to her father and brothers. Often it is the girl's father, rather than the suitor himself, who suggests that the couple get married. Lapsed is the ancient custom of a suitor bringing the girl the liver of a freshly killed tapir or spider monkey for her to roast (she rejected him by refusing to cook it). A proposal today might go something like this:

"Would you like to live with me, Potential Wife?"

"Yes, I would like to live with you."

"Then, come on, let's go right now."

"All right, let's do."

Obviously the situation must somehow have been decided earlier: the man appears assured of the answer he will receive.

As all this activity over eleven-year-old Pacho indicated, there is an intense shortage of women amongst the Amahuaca, and the demand for mates results in girls getting married much earlier than boys. The great majority of girls marry before they reach puberty, usually between the ages of eight and eleven, though the availability of a mate appears to be the basic determinant for marriage regardless of a partner's age, kinship relationships, and parental wishes. While it is certainly more common to find a man of twenty-five or thirty marrying a girl of eight or ten, it is not difficult to find examples of age disparities in reverse: Coyaso's mother is at least fifteen years senior to her present husband. Far rarer is marriage between two children. Such an event occurred three years ago when a couple "adopted" a six-year-old girl, after her mother had been widowed by a hunting accident, and made her the "wife" of their two-year-old boy. The girl is little more than a slave, babysitting her "husband" and fetching and carrying for her mother-in-law. Even by Amahuaca standards the boy is absurdly young to be married; this is a case of child peonage, rather than of child marriage.

When Pansitimba looks around the families gathered at Varadero and their relatives on the Curiuja, he can see that there is no girl immediately available to him. While he keeps repeating that he does not intend to get married for a long, long time, it is more than likely that this man-boy is rather unhappy over his prospects. His brother, barely two years his senior, is already married and a father; Pacho's brother, who is only three years older, is also married. Nevertheless, Pansitimba is not the only one seeking a wife at Varadero: both his maternal uncle (whose quirk it was to have built himself a totally closed, beehive hut unlike any other in the neighborhood) and the charming but irresponsible Coyaso are bachelors who live alone—and hate it.

In this society that so strictly demarcates work patterns, the single man is in a highly uncomfortable position. He finds that he must depend upon the good will of his female relatives to fill the needs he cannot meet himself: maize and manioc, the pots to cook them in, the cotton thread for assembling his arrows. It is only when it comes to sex that the single Amahuaca is not frustrated, since his society grants him sexual access to all of his brothers' wives, a social device known as the "anticipatory levirate." Nevertheless the pressures to find a wife are immense.

This dearth of women is the result of female infanticide and polygyny. These social practices are so pervasive that one cannot help but wonder whether the Amahuaca—like some of the other Montaña tribes—may not eventually disappear. Russell, who has discussed this with the Varadero group, reports that "the Amahuaca do not seem to be very much concerned. . . . They say, 'Yes,' with a smile, 'pretty soon there will not be any Amahuaca.'" Neither polygyny nor female infanticide is limited to them; both are indigenous to most of the Montaña Indians. And the resulting shortage of women is considered by most observers to have been a prime cause for much of the intertribal and intervillage warfare once endemic in this region.

Female infanticide establishes an original over-all shortage of women; polygyny worsens the imbalance. Thus Maxoopo as well as his three brothers have more than one wife; between them these four men have taken eleven women out of circulation. Polygyny frequently starts when a man marries two sisters. And quite a number of the polygynous households have been established through marriage with a dead brother's widow—the classical levirate of the Old Testament and a custom practiced the world around.

Maxoopo's youngest brother, Tumonno, is a case in point. Of Tumonno's four wives, two bear a somewhat complicated relationship to Tumonno's murdered brother, Ishman. Tumonno's first wife was ten years old when they were married—a rather loveless union apparently, which was undertaken only because there was no other girl available at the time. Thus when Tumonno married his second wife, he gave the first one to Ishman, and she became the latter's second wife. After Ishman was killed a few years later, Tumonno took over the two surviving widows, one of whom was the wife he had originally given away.

Tumonno's fourth wife is also his niece, and she offers an example of why taboos exist on certain types of consanguinous relationships. Since each wife of any family of brothers is sexually available to all the brothers, marriage between a woman and her paternal uncle is prohibited—he might easily have sired her. Since Tumonno's last wife is technically his brother Maxoopo's daughter, Tumonno might well have been marrying his own daughter. Actually, the quiet gossip around Varadero has it that the girl was really fathered by the murdered brother, Ishman, Tumonno's paternity being only attributed to this girl's youngest sister.

There is a wide gap between what the Amahuaca preach and what they practice in terms of incest. Having merely casual sexual relations with an individual within a prohibited kinship category is apparently not viewed as incest. Indeed, most children seem to have their first sexual experiences with siblings, and such experimentation is not considered a violation of taboos. To be considered incestuous (and disapproved) the relationship must include one adult partner and be maintained long enough for the couple to be considered "married." However, sanctions are not enforced against transgressors.

If sibling incest is fairly common at Varadero, less common is the practice of a man marrying mother and daughter at the same time. Maxoopo's marriage to Rohanhno, which apparently also included her eldest daughter, is the only reported case, though the variant of marrying mother and daughter seriatim is quite well known. The practice of permanently exchanging spouses is also rare; the only example is that of an uncle of Pansitimba, who, in a shuffle that has proved eminently successful, exchanged wives with his cousin and good friend. Relations between the four are most cordial.

All these permutations and combinations that so obviously disregard taboo kinship relationships in marriage should not imply that Amahuaca adults have unlimited sexual freedom. Extramarital affairs—if one excludes those socially sanctioned within the anticipatory levirate—often signal the end of a marriage. For the adulterous wife will most likely get a sound thrashing when her husband discovers the state of her affairs. Such beatings may be severe enough to keep her in her hammock for a few days, and while little opprobrium is attached to the event (women will frequently laugh and talk about their beatings), a wife will not put up with much of this. The dissolution of a marriage is a frequent, almost normal, event and is most likely to occur early in life and during the first years of a union. Such "divorces" take place even though the woman may have one or two children. However, the likelihood of a breakup greatly decreases with the number of children involved and the duration of the marriage. Before she remarries, a divorcée or a widow with children from a previous marriage will frequently give them away for adoption, usually to a relative. Sometimes after she has settled down with her new husband, she may try to claim her children, though whether or not they are returned depends on how useful they are around the foster home.

Apart from death, marriages may break up because one partner may find the other lazy or incompetent or promiscuous. One of Pansitimba's uncles turned his wife out, claiming that she was lazy and because she refused to follow him downstream. This is, however, one of the few cases on record in which a husband has divested himself of a wife. Usually the woman walks out on her husband.

MUCH LOVE goes into bringing up an Amahuaca child. Intimate physical contact between mother and child is continuous: the infant is carried everywhere in a sling; it sleeps on its mother's lap while she does many of her chores; it will be in her hammock at night until it is three years old. A child is suckled not only to give it food, for women who have little, if any, milk will give their breast to a fretting child, to a frightened one, to a child they want to put to sleep. It is the Perfect Anodyne of childhood, and I have seen a boy of eight being reassured at his grandmother's teat. The extended family, too, obviously plays a significant role in offering a child warmth, affection, conviviality, a feeling of belonging. Yet odd as it may seem by Western standards, all this is quietly done, with no great outward show of emotion or flow of verbiage: a gesture here, a hug there; a little bow made for a young hunter, a clay doll for a girl. To an Amahuaca child, they all spell out the adults' love for him.

Discipline is rarely physically enforced by parents, and a child's right to assert himself, his right to choose, is fundamentally accepted. Younger children seem usually to be physically disciplined by their older siblings. Pansitimba, one evening, administered a well-deserved thumping to his incorrigible younger brother for being obstreperous at a social gathering. His parents all the while looked on, murmuring appreciative comments now and again, but took no active role in this learning process. However fighting between children of different families is definitely not encouraged. Indeed, if a child fights with other children, his parents will scold him and may even switch his legs.

Spanking children is practically unheard of, as Russell found out. One of Rohanhno's boys had a fixation on digging holes in the airstrip, and despite Russell's oft-repeated explanation to both parents and child that these holes endangered the planes, the boy continued to dig them. Catching him at his work one day, Russell managed to get in a couple of whacks on the bottom as the boy was running away, and the ensuing yells brought his parents on the run from their *chacra*. As Russell records it:

"Rohanhno said, 'You don't know how painful it is to give birth to a child. Now that you have spanked my son, he will become skinny and die.'

"While Maxoopo made a scene, waving his machete: 'You spanked my son, didn't you?' he asked. 'I'm going to beat up on you. If it were not for these visitors, I'd do it right now.'

"The thought went through my mind," Russell continues, "that I should fight it out with Maxoopo, since he wouldn't listen to reason. 'Big M' (as we often refer to him) was very muscular." (This last is a vast understatement, for while the Amahuaca have no chief, Maxoopo is far and away the most impressive of them all: a big, scarred man with a bull neck, a barrel chest, and a deep resonant voice to match. Certainly not a nice customer to tangle with, particularly with a machete in hand.)

Needless to say, Russell did not tangle with Maxoopo, not because of the man's strength, since Russell thought his wrestling experience might make up for some of the other's muscles, but because he felt that this was no way to settle the problem.

Switching usually stops by the time the child is about eight years of age. Occasionally adults will discipline a disobedient child with a horrid plant called *ishishmua* which raises a most unpleasant and painful welt. Pansitimba's impossible younger brother during a visit to an aunt one day kept on meddling with his aunt's belongings despite her repeated warnings. She finally lost patience and cut a sprig of this noxious plant, which she then placed on the items the pest had been told not to touch. This time, when he went after them, he received a painful lesson.

In the case of very young children, mothers will threaten them with: "If you do (don't do) thus and such, you'll get diarrhea." And since diarrhea is a most objectionable disorder, the outrageous lie might have some effect. A somewhat less outrageous statement came from a mother trying to get her child to return from his solitary exploration of a *chacra:* she yelled that snakes and jaguars skulked there.

The Amahuaca child's world seems extraordinarily free of controls to Western eyes. Equally very few attempts are made to protect youngsters from any except the most dangerous of hazards—such as snakes in tall grass, or falling off a cliff—and tiny tots play with knives or handle live coals at an age where any Western parent would rush to their "protection." Even respect for age, which colors much of Amahuaca social relationships, is not rigidly enforced upon children, particularly the very young. I have seen Pansitimba's brother lift a leg while emitting a Bronx cheer to show his contempt for an adult. However, as the child gets older he becomes more cautious, for if he gets too bumptious, an older sibling will eventually bestir himself to whack some manners into the offender.

Children will be shamed into action, as was Pansitimba's younger brother on one occasion. Coyaso had asked him to fetch a papaya, and when he refused, sulking, Pansitimba got it. Coyaso taunted the lout, saying that he was bad while Pansitimba was good; that he was dead; that he had a belly fat from intestinal parasites; and that Pansitimba was a handsome man because he had been willing to run an errand for him. He went on at some length and apparently shamed the boy successfully, for a few days afterward the child was seen going off to help Coyaso poison fish.

Toilet training starts early, and a mother will shake or scold a baby who urinates or defecates on her. Only when a child is old enough to walk do his parents show him the special hole they have prepared for him in the general lavatory area near the house, and tell him that he must void there and nowhere else. Should he want to urinate at night, his mother takes him outside, reminding him that all he has to do is to notify her of his needs. Lapses on his part may get him a slap or two; if he persists, a switching on the back of his calves. I was amused to see Pacho play with a small puppy much as if it were a baby, carrying it in a sling and pretending to nurse it. Every once in a while she would tickle its belly till it urinated—the same thing that is done to a very young infant.

Children get bathed early. If the child is very young and the river particularly cold, the mother will take a mouthful of water so as to warm it up and gently spray the child with it. A child's hair is searched for lice, and then it is slicked down with spit. Nails are trimmed by being carefully torn off or bitten off, after which the toilet is completed by painting the infant with *huito* (a dark purple-black stain) as a disease repellent, or by dusting it all over with ashes as an insect repellent. An infant is introduced to solid foods around six months of age (*muto* or manioc or roasted banana). These are well chewed by the mother who spits the mash into the infant's mouth. (Young animals are also fed in this way: Pansitimba took a handful of *muto* and, after chewing it for a little while, fed Pacho's puppy, mouth to muzzle.)

When a woman decides to wean a child, she will rub the fruit of an *ají* vine on her nipples. This must have a catastrophic impact, for this devilish red pepper will set any mouth afire. No wonder children are weaned.

AS A GENERAL RULE an Amahuaca woman gives birth unassisted, though a mother may help her daughter, particularly if it is a first birth. A woman will go off into the brush and deliver the baby by herself, and then return to the house to continue most of her regular chores. Maxoopo's first wife, for example, had a child when all the other adults in her clearing were away visiting. The Russells found her grinding corn, carrying water, and doing the rest of the household work within a couple of hours after having given birth.

Husbands have nothing to do with the process and indeed seem uneasy about the whole thing. Thus Jawachiwayamba's married stepson, Mananyamba, appeared at the Russells' door one morning and hung around without doing anything or saying much of why he was there. Soon after he left, one of the women reported that his wife, Munsho, had just given birth—Mananyamba obviously had cleared out. It was by no means a usual birth, as the Russells discovered later. For Munsho had had twins, an event that is looked upon with considerable disfavor, particularly by the mother.

Munsho, a young woman of sixteen, is small even by Amahuaca standards. Pretty but petulant, her first child was barely toddling when the twins were born. When I saw Munsho, the twins were about six months old, both little girls, but there the resemblance ended. While one was a lively infant, a cheerful little animal that climbed all over its mother, the other was thin and gray, crying interminably in a despairing whine. She was so weak that she could barely keep her mouth on Munsho's nipple, and her mother was continually having to push the infant's head back into position.

That either of the twins is alive today is solely due to the Russells' efforts and their obvious unhappiness over the Amahuaca's propensity to commit infanticide. The reason that the babies had not been strangled was simple: Munsho, knowing of the Russells' feelings, had saved the twins as a gift for the missionaries. Luckily this information got back to them before the offer could be made, so that Russell was able to intercept Mananyamba to tell him that they had no desire to deprive the Amahuaca of their children. And besides, the Russells were quite satisfied with the size of their own family. These remarks effectively shut off any talk of adoption.

However, the twins still had to be kept alive, which was quite a problem because they weighed no more than four pounds each. Matters were further complicated when, a week after their birth, the parents decided to make a trip downriver, leaving one infant with its grandmother. The Russells discovered this only on the day of departure, and when they protested that the grandmother had no milk, the old lady was outraged. She graphically demonstrated her capacity by squeezing her breasts, sending jets of liquid halfway across the hut! In the face of such prowess there was little that the Russells could say, and Mananyamba and his family set off downstream. Within a few days, however, the grandmother came to the Russells for help: the infant was near death from starvation. Mrs. Russell, with powdered milk, an eyedropper, and vast effort, managed to keep her alive until Munsho returned.

For this single case of infanticide prevented, there are many, many more examples of women killing their newborn. Five infants alone were killed by the two women of Maxoopo's household. Like Munsho, Rohanhno also had twins. In her case, however, it was her mother who killed them. "I was so frightened to see two babies appear, instead of just one, that I buried them," she said. (The old lady herself admits to strangling two of her own.) As for Maxoopo's first wife, she almost certainly killed three. (She told the Russells with a smile: "I would have strangled this one also," pointing to Pacho, "but her grandmother wouldn't let me.") Infanticide is not viewed by the Amahuaca as murder, for newborns are not considered human beings, but rather little animals. Indeed, babies are named after they are a year old—only after their chances of survival seem assured.

The decision to kill a newborn may be made before the woman goes off into the brush to deliver; or it may be made right after the child is born. It is usually the mother who decides to do so after finding that it is not of the desired sex (male), that it is a multiple birth, or that it doesn't look like a nice child. Only occasionally is burial resorted to; usually the woman ties a vine around the infant's neck and throws the little corpse out into the brush. As in all matters pertaining to childbirth, the father is practically never consulted in this. He pretends to ignorance: should he be asked his wife's intentions, he will reply, "I don't know. You'll have to ask her." And should the woman return from her delivery without a newborn, he will continue blandly to profess his ignorance of what occurred.

79

There are no special rituals surrounding birth: the umbilical cord is tied off with a vine or a piece of cotton, the placenta is thrown away or buried, and the mother washes herself off in a stream before going home. There she usually takes it somewhat easy for two or three days, undertaking only the lighter household chores. Neither are there major taboos surrounding gestation or childbirth: while the pregnant woman is not supposed to eat tortoise, tapir, or armadillo, such sanctions are rarely obeyed. Again, the father-to-be has no restraints placed upon him; for, unlike most of the Montaña Indian men, he keeps on hunting the same game and eating the foods he always did.

WHILE neither the process of weaving nor the finished material is particularly interesting, threadmaking certainly is. Cuho, who is one of the best weavers in Varadero, uses an almost magical series of patterned gestures to spin thread: I have sat a half-hour at a time, literally entranced, watching her. Spearing a cotton boll upon a foot-long spindle, she beats it on her forearm until it becomes an airy dough-nut of fluff, so light that the merest hint of a breath would blow it away. Then, gathering the puff of cotton in her left hand, she pinches it onto the tail end of a thread already on her toplike spindle, which she sets to twirling in a bowl. And now, in a long, slow, gliding motion older than man's art and more stylized than any ballerina's gesture, she plays out the fluff through her thumb and forefinger, where it suddenly becomes thread, keeping an even tension as she stretches out her left arm to its fullest extension. It is this last gesture—this almost magical opening of herself, with wrist finely bent, and fingers tuned to the least variations in the fiber—that keeps me motionless, fearful that any distraction would make her break the gossamer that appears so wondrously from between her fingers.

All other operations—from the first fluffing out of the cotton boll to the final return swoop, during which the thread is searched out for imperfections before it is wound onto the spindle—are but the practiced motions, the unconscious pyrotechnics, of any skilled artisan working at his trade.

Thickness of thread is determined by the degree to which the boll is fluffed; threads may be twisted together to form strings which, in turn, may be twisted together to form cord. Thread size varies, depending upon what the woman is weaving or tying. A woman's skirt, for example, is woven from a heavy, multiple thread; a hammock is twined from cord; while the very finest cotton thread is woven into strips of cloth for use as bracelets above the elbows and below the knee, or for decorating their top hats.

An Amahuaca child gets his first clothing after being weaned: a mother will weave a skirt for her daughter when she is about three; a boy will have his first penis string at about the same age. This, too, is usually the time when a child's nasal septum is pierced for the ornament that nearly all Amahuaca sport. Originally this ornament was made from a triangular piece of tortoise shell or mother-of-pearl cut from the shell of a large freshwater mussel; then, around the turn of the century, when rubber gatherers first penetrated this region, the Amahuaca substituted silver coins. Today the disks are made from aluminum cut from the body of an S. I. L. plane which crashed near the airstrip. Progress! Progress!

Close to a generation ago the Amahuaca wore feathers stuck in holes pierced in the ears and around the mouth. This is no longer the fashion, and only amongst the older men and women can feather holes still be seen. Nasal disks are also going out of vogue: Pansitimba does not have one, and the parents of a number of the younger children have indicated they will not make their children wear them.

It is curious that, despite their proficiency as weavers, and their knowledge of a variety of natural dyestuffs, the Amahuaca only very, very rarely weave designs into their cloth. Even then, the decoration is extraordinarily simple, the material being woven in parallel bands of white and red-brown, the threads for the latter dyed with the juice of mahogany bark. More frequently, a woman works *achiote* paste into the material she has woven, giving it a brilliant brick color overall. But there is no attempt, either during the weaving itself or on the finished material, to be at all fanciful. Such artistic expression is found primarily in Amahuaca body decoration.

AMAHUACA BODY PAINT comes from two fruits: the bright red-orange *achiote*, and the dense purple-black *huito*. In addition to its decorative purposes, *achiote* is considered an insect repellent. It is then used as a decorative undercoat, being mixed with liquefied fat from a tapir or spider monkey to prevent it from drying out. Fat is a fine medium when fresh, but when rancid.... One day when one of the men appeared with a newly applied coat, I was driven out of the hut, so pervasive was the stench. The poor chap soon couldn't stand it himself and tried hard to wash it off, but the smell lingered on. We eventually had to give him a piece of soap and a nail brush before we could stand him upwind. Occasionally *achiote* will be used as the primary make-up: for instance, when the men hold a party to commune with ghosts, each man will paint a mask upon his own face by measuring off equal distances from eyes, nose, and mouth to achieve a symmetrical design.

More usual, however, is a very elaborate face make-up, when everybody practices his talents on someone else. *Huito*, in contrast to *achiote*, is used as decoration (though babies are frequently painted from head to toe with it to ward off disease); the designs vary from Jackson Pollock squiggles, produced by squeezing the fruit till it dribbles deliciously down chest and arms and legs, to carefully applied patterns on the face. Until Russell brought in mirrors, the narcissistic pleasures of the make-up artist must have been somewhat frustrated: he could apply his most creative talents only to the decoration of others.

While there are some classic designs—traditional face mask patterns with such names as "tiger" (jaguar), or "catfish" which may tie in with long-lost animistic beliefs or kinship groupings—most of the decoration is purely cosmetic, and the fanciful expressions of the artist contain no inherent meanings of their own. Arms and legs may get jaguarlike splotches or ripples (these are applied with a cotton-boll daub), while the face receives a careful geometric design (applied with a thin reed), usually running in a triangle from ear to ear, crossing over the tip of the nose. A solid black area around the lips, rather like Pierrot's tragic mouth, and a series of straight lines and dots horizontally across the forehead and cheekbones complete the picture.

There is only one time when body decoration has any real significance, and that is when a man has murder on his mind: then he will paint himself black all over, crop his hair, make himself a set of barbed "killer" arrows, and go off to ambush his victim. Amahuaca seeing a man so got up become very frightened and keep their weapons at the ready until he has gone by.

While there have been reports that the Amahuaca used to tattoo their faces (using a palm-thorn needle and rubbing dye into the puncture), only Jawachi-wayamba's first wife is so marked. This technique is otherwise unknown to the group at Varadero.

There is much enjoyment in painting and dressing up, and the slightest excuse suffices: social occasions, the arrival of a party from the Curiuja, visitors to the Russells, or merely the decision to hold a song fest will bring out the top hats, tails, and cummerbunds of the men and the ladies' best sheath skirts and bead necklaces. The top hats are made from the inner layers of bamboo covered by strips of finely woven cloth soaked with *achiote*. Stitched all around the cloth cover are black and brown seeds, interspersed with monkey teeth. Two, three, sometimes four (once I even counted five) layers of cloth and beads may be sewed to the hat, which has a coarse red fringe of shredded bast masking the eyes. The men are an impressive sight as they walk about solemnly, their bark penis belts hidden beneath an enormous seed stomacher, which may reach forty yards in length, and a knee-fringe skirt of cotton strings dyed red. But the illusion of dignity is soon shattered:

The nasal disk, once made from tortoise shell or mother-of-pearl from a freshwater mussel, is today of aluminum from a crashed supply plane. Pansitimba being painted by his mother; a man's leg is decorated by his wife.

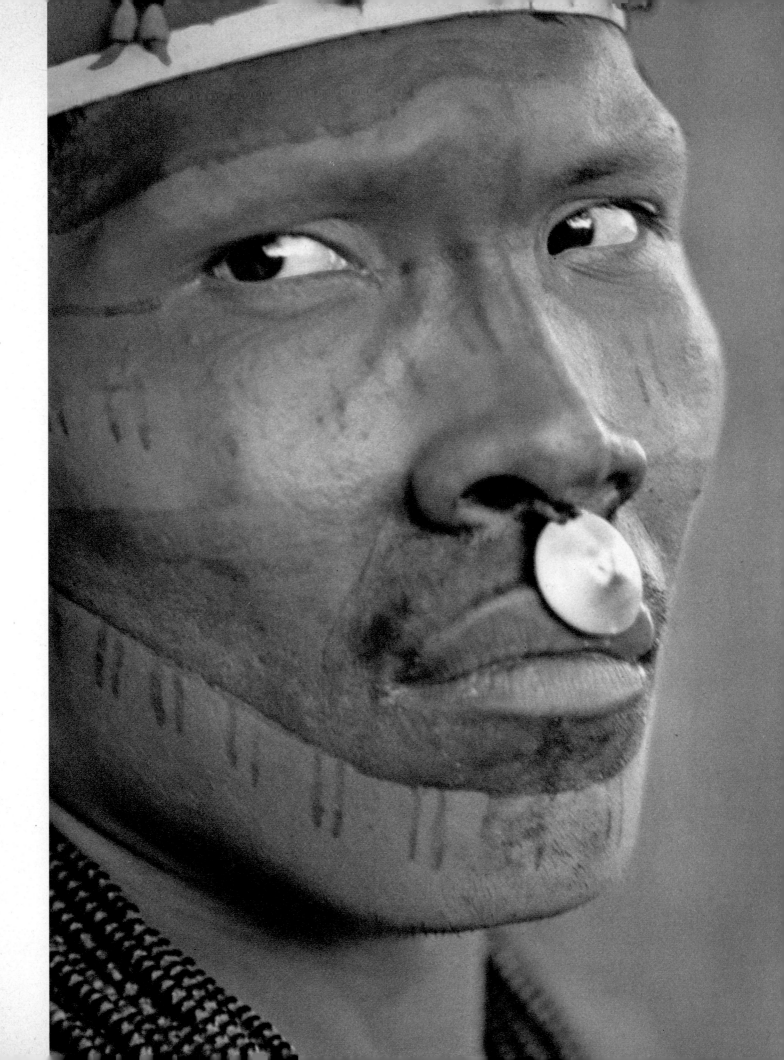

hats take on a raffish tilt, the seed stomachers need to be continually adjusted through an elaborate series of coilings and uncoilings, while the fringe skirts bring back the memory of brawny female impersonators at university smokers.

One of the more curious aspects of Amahuaca life is the absence of what I call "decorative elaboration": of their technology, their persons, their social relationships—in short, the arts. Unlike most other Indian cultures of the Montaña, one of the most noticeable—even remarkable—features of the Amahuaca is the poverty of their arts. Quite apart from being technically primitive and unimaginative, astonishingly few elements of their daily lives receive any decorative attention. This is true of their technology (for example, weaving and pottery are rarely distinguished by any designs; only arrow points commonly receive such attention); and of their dress (hats and headbands are the only items that get a dash of paint; and apart from a rare feather plume on a headband, their bracelets, necklaces, stomachers, and hats employ only two different kinds of seed and perhaps, on occasion, a few animal teeth).

Where is the elegant weaving and cloth painting produced by some of the other Montaña Indians? The imaginative glazing of pots? The decorated bows with multicolored arrows? The shaped and incised mortars, stools, benches, paddles? The fabulous feather and insect dress decorations? The Amahuaca certainly don't produce any of these.

This same lack of decoration is equally notable in Amahuaca social relations—the ceremonious and social aspects of their arts—dance, song, and music. Compared with the other tribes of the Montaña, these are not merely unelaborated, but also quite infrequent; and they are primarily spontaneous rather than planned. Dancing, under whatever circumstances, involves but four figures (a circle, a circle within a circle, a straight line, and two lines face to face); three steps (shuffle right and shuffle left, a front-and-back, a leap); and but one beat (all rhythms are stepped out) without unison (so long as the rhythm is stepped, it matters not a whit which foot is used). Their singing shows the same lack of complication. It is always homophonic and unaccompanied, frequently with leader and chorus in ritornel; and chanted rather than sung (often not in unison) in a tonal range no greater than that of the speaking voice (less than two octaves). Rhythm is barely accentuated, and there are no drums, hand claps, gourds, or rattles; the beat is a simple 2:2 or 4:4. Musically the songs are endless, infinitely simple variations on four or five notes with no discernible melody, the scale (if there be one) probably pentatonic. As can be imagined, a night-long song fest is to Western ears unutterably boring. What few musical instruments there are must be viewed as toys, rather than as serious mechanisms for making music. A three-holed recorder, a bark trumpet, and a single-string "mouth bow" strummed with the midrib of a palm leaflet comprise the entire inventory.

Why should a catalogue of Amahuaca arts be so extraordinarily small in comparison with some of the other Montaña Indians? In large part, I feel sure, it stems from the dispersed nature of Amahuaca society. Until Russell established Varadero as a safe haven, a neutral territory, the Amahuaca were jungle nomads, moving every three or four years. Rarely did more than three families group together even for this short space of time, for they preferred to live alone, a day or more apart. Artistic expression, therefore, has not been stimulated by either locus or tradition. Such isolation also reduces the opportunity for emulation and vastly limits the size of any interested and appreciative audience. This lack of arts certainly cannot be due to the pressures of making a living, for the Amahuaca have a great deal of leisure time, much of which they occupy with nonproductive labor: the energy expended in collecting, drilling, and stringing the twenty-odd thousand seeds that make up a man's stomacher is fantastic. But this really is make-work to fill time. For while these belts are admittedly decoration, they cannot really be considered an art form, since there is no attempt to vary color, size, or shape.

Much of the leisure time—and most of this is man's, not woman's leisure time—is spent merely sitting around. A man may sit puffing on his pipe (though this is usually reserved for company), or talking to other people (if there are some around). Most conversations are unbelievably banal: minutiae about hunting, or the behavior (usually Rabelaisian) of a certain dog, or why so many pots were found broken in the last batch a woman fired. Such accounts are listened to with enormous interest and generate lively responses. I could never get over the fact that what appeared to be deep, even passionate interchanges, were but endless and sterile recapitulations of trivia.

However, if a man is alone, he just sits there blankly in "no time." Perhaps he may scrape down a callus on the sole of his foot, or dig out an old thorn, or trim his nails. But more often he just sits doing nothing, looking at nothing, and, I'm sure, thinking about nothing. I don't remember ever seeing a bored Amahuaca, though I've seen any number of them in "no time" being blank, as if they had gone into a kind of hibernation. Boredom, indeed, is a civilized disease, stemming from the necessity of having to make choices between socially sanctioned unessential ways of spending time away from survival activities. In a society where survival— that is, not going hungry, or wet, or naked—occupies but part of a man's time; a society where decorative elaboration as a means of passing time is extraordinarily limited; a society, in short, where the concept of spending (leisure) time doesn't exist since there is nothing to spend it on, there is no alternative but to go blank.

Despite their extreme cleanliness, the Amahuaca sometimes get head lice. Sitting around in "no time."

Exactly how limited is the decorative elaboration of Amahuaca group relations? Well, there are no marriage or birth rites; no taboos associated with pregnancy; no puberty trials for either boys or girls; groups of men do not make hunting magics in a formalized ritual way (though a man may occasionally, and privately, try to conjure success in the chase); the shaman as a public, professional role, doesn't exist; and since the Amahuaca have not as yet become organized as a community, there is no warfare mystagogy. A man will go out and kill a personal enemy, alone or perhaps with the assistance of a couple of relatives, but never as a member of an organized war party. The only ceremonious occasions are two harvest festivals, which are held most infrequently, their ritual barely formalized, and the fairly common binges with the hallucinating drug *ayahuasca*, during which souls are summoned and consulted on various matters.

THIS EVENING we have a fire going in front of our hut and have put benches around. Amahuaca from across the airstrip drift over by ones and twos, their faint musky-geranium smell almost lost in the scent of the lime tree that blooms behind the hut. A vast full moon, improbably bright orange, is rising over the hut, and I unconsciously brace myself for Lowell Thomas's voice. One of the children—probably Pansitimba's impossible young brother—has brought along a goggle-eyed cicada to play with, and so loudly does it squeal that the ethnologists, who plan to use their tape recorder, have to call for its liquidation. For tonight we are going to hear an Amahuaca story.

The role of public storyteller, like that of shaman, does not exist amongst the Amahuaca, for storytelling is not a public event. Myths seem to have no emotional overtones and are not incorporated into any ceremonies, and most stories are told within the family, rarely to so large a group as this one. Even the best of storytellers may forget details, but this is not important, for someone is sure to supply them: the myths are obviously well known. As a storyteller Pansitimba's father is no great shakes, having a low mumbly voice and a forgetful disposition, so the following account includes a considerable number of helpful interjections from the rest of the audience:

"Hindachindiya was the first Amahuaca man. He had no wife and lived with his mother. He went and got a *sapalla* fruit and copulated with it, but all the children he had by it rotted. So he told his mother to bring him a *xopa* fruit, whereupon he copulated with it. The *xopa* became pregnant. It became large and black. He put it in his hammock and told his mother to be careful with it. But in sweeping the house one day, she was clumsy and bumped the hammock. The fruit fell to the ground and broke open, spilling out two babies, a boy and a girl. The boy died; the girl lived. She was the first Amahuaca woman. The mother of Hindachindiya brought up the girl, and when she was old enough, Hindachindiya married her; there were no other Amahuaca women. Their children were the first Amahuaca children, and all Amahuaca today are descended from them.

"Hindachindiya was fabulously endowed. Whenever he felt like making love, he would send his penis out to the house of the woman he wanted. When he had finished, he would call it back and coil it around his neck for safekeeping. When he died, it was cut into small pieces and thrown into the river. These became *cunchi* (catfish) and caused all the fish to multiply."

Hindachindiya's world is a curious place, where time holds no meaning, where the birds and beasts and fish possess anthropomorphic natures, and where a man is as ready to mate with them as with a woman. It is a world supported on tree roots which keep it from sinking into the primordial waters; a world that has suffered Flood, Fire, and Quake. (Curiously enough, the world has not been created: it always was, and the creation myth does not appear to exist.)

After Hindachindiya had populated the world with Amahuaca, the sky fell down upon Earth which shuddered to its roots at the blow. Huuo, the toad, was finally able to push it back into place, but Earth was so crushed that the primordial waters ran back up the rivers, flooded the land, and drowned most of the animals. In order to escape the cataclysm, all the Amahuaca, save one couple, took on the form of trumpeter birds, but these all perished, being eaten one by one by *yoshi* (ghosts). However, the couple survived by copying the Hero, Rantanga, who made himself a pair of spider monkey boots with which he climbed to the top of the tallest tree of the forest. Eventually the waters receded, and the couple were able to raise a family—only to be threatened once again by a holocaust that wiped out nearly all living things. It had inadvertently been set by Squirrel who had stolen fire from the family in order to burn off his *chacra*, where it got out of hand.

This series of traumatic events seems to have left the family with a case of collective amnesia. They wandered about, eating only nuts and fruits and grubs, for they had forgotten everything. Luckily, Rantanga found them. He taught them how to make pots and log trough mortars; how to clear their gardens and plant maize and manioc; how to make bows and arrows and stone axes; how to hunt and fish. Rantanga taught the Amahuaca how to do all these things at a place called Maino-a, at the headwaters of the Purús where he lived on an island with his wife, Ata. (There is some confusion as to the exact role that Rantanga holds in the genealogy of the Amahuaca, since many of the group at Varadero believe that all of the Amahuaca descended from him rather than from that fine Rabelaisian hero, Hindachindiya.) Rantanga finally died and went to heaven. His *yoshi* used to attend the Amahuaca's maize and banana ceremonies, but no longer does so. Rantanga's only manifestation in today's world is that of thunder: the noise he makes in clearing his heavenly *chacras*.

THE MORE ONE LISTENS to the Amahuaca myths, the clearer it is that they are really a series of unconnected episodes, that they do not form an organized mythology. Certainly there is no chronology to them. It is not possible to determine whether the holocaust came before or after the falling heavens, or who really was the progenitor of the Amahuaca. Some of the Amahuaca myths are obviously variants of themes common to all of the Indians of the Montaña, such as the Hindachindiya penis motif, or the tale of the *wandati yoshi*, frog women whose vaginas were lined with teeth. (While both the vagina dentata and the penis transfixus motifs are to be found the world across, the particular details of the Hindachindiya and the *wandati yoshi* myths are characteristically repeated by quite a number of the other Montaña tribes.) Other myths of the Amahuaca have elements common to far larger groupings than the people of the Montaña. The arrow-chain motif, known to Indian cultures of both North and South America, is found in the Amahuaca story about the Sons of Oxu, the Moon, and his sister Wunta, and how they finally go to heaven. After innumerable adventures three of the four brothers stopped to invent bows and arrows and then decided to try them out by shooting into the sky. When one arrow finally went high enough to lodge there, the boys continued to shoot; and such was their miraculous aim that the point of one arrow found its mark in the butt end of the previous one, until they formed a chain reaching from Earth to Sky. Up this chain the brothers sent a small red squirrel to throw them down a ladder, by which the three finally reached Heaven (the fourth became a bird and remained on Earth). There you can see them today, for they form one of the major constellations, our Pleiades.

Tracing out Amahuaca constellations brings out a number of star figures in common with the configurations of the Western world: Orion, Delphinus, Aquila, and the zodiacal figures of Scorpio, Taurus, Aries, and Sagittarius.

In addition, the Amahuaca have delineated two other major constellations: the jaguar chasing a deer, and Wishituku, the one-legged man, facing a crocodile's head. Wishituku, say the Amahuaca, was leading his people to heaven (for they had become tired of fighting off dangerous animals) when they came to a lake in which basked a vast cayman. Wishituku sent his people tiptoeing safely across the sleeping animal, but when it was his turn he forgot his own instructions. His stomping woke up the crocodile who threw him into the water and bit off his leg before he could get to shore. Nevertheless he and his tribe did get to heaven, and there he sits facing the beast to which he owes his amputation while his people crowd about him. The remaining constellations form a collection of storyless odds and ends: a monkey's eye, four cooking fires (which Wishituku brought up for his people), a hunter's blind from which to shoot small birds.

In this simple mythology of the Amahuaca there are clearly no supernatural beings powerful enough nor exalted enough to be called gods.

Harvest festivals might be considered traditional in that the average Amahuaca knows their general form. However, it would seem that they do not hold any deep social significance, since only two have been held in Varadero during the past decade. Indeed, quite a number of the adults privately admitted that they had never observed or participated in this type of ceremony. Actually the term "harvest festival" is a misnomer. While these ceremonies are held at a time when the maize and bananas have ripened, they have nothing to do with either propitiating or thanking supernatural powers for the crop. Neither are they fertility ceremonies. They are held, insofar as it can be determined, not to make the children grow up to become strong men or fertile women, but just to grow up quickly.

While the actual ceremony of the banana festival took less than half a morning, the preliminary activities spanned an entire month and put the participants to quite some trouble. There were well over three hundred hours of group singing during this time, and since most of it took place after sundown, the small community enjoyed very little sleep. Singing lasted from dusk to three in the morning, sometimes from dusk to dawn. Rarely was there less than six hours of song, and only five nights passed without a voice being raised.

While all of the adults at Varadero—plus a number of their immediate kinfolk living near by—participated in the ceremony, it was planned, organized, and executed solely by the two "owners" of the feast—a term that needs some explanation. In some South American jungle tribes the "ownership" of a feast is hereditary, combining the concept of copyright holder with sponsor, and gives the individual considerable prestige. Amongst the Kuikuru of Brazil, for example, there are seventeen such traditional feasts, each with its separate owner, who may, if he wishes, sell this privilege outright. The owner of the feast holds the final voice in determining if and when it shall be held and is obliged to supply and cook the necessary ingredients. However, another individual is impresario for the shindig. He sounds out the temper of the village on the merits of holding the feast, rounds up the performers who traditionally serve a particular ceremony, and in general acts as m.c. for the whole proceedings.

Amongst the Amahuaca the ownership of a festival is not a hereditary right. Rumor has it that the upriver families rotate ownership amongst various individuals; at Varadero it is apparently assumed at will. Thus Maxoopo and Jawachiwayamba announced one spring that they were claiming ownership of a banana festival which they intended to call in the fall. But they never did, and when the festival was eventually held a couple of years later, it was under different sponsorship. Clearly, then, neither ownership of a feast nor the feast itself carries much prestige amongst the Amahuaca.

The success of the banana festival was due to the experience of one of the owners, a recent arrival at Varadero. This man had twice gone through the ceremony in recent years and was an efficient organizer to boot. Somehow he managed to make the little community at Varadero really believe that they would be plagued by ill fortune should they refuse to join the ceremony: poisonous snakes would bite them, their children would not grow up. Russell reports that at one time or another most of the participants in the ceremony had come to him to say that they would never cooperate in another such feast—it was just too much work.

The preparations for a banana ceremony are simple, if drawn out, being designed to hasten the ripening of the bananas (actually plantains, since they are the green cooking variety). The songs detail the owners' plans to hold the feast, announce who is on their guest list, describe the work of harvesting, and recount the steps involved in preparing the final banana brew. Much of this singing is accompanied by dances in which the participants act out the words of the songs. Thus a guest receives his invitation when the owners come singing and dancing up to his hut, where they shoot him with *taa tucus,* arrows whose heads have been removed and replaced by pads of banana leaves. Since such a "special delivery" obviously cannot be ignored, the guest immediately returns his R.S.V.P. in person by joining the owners as they dance off to the next hut. Along with those of his hosts, he lets fly his own *taa tucu* upon the next guest in line, and so on.

There was no escaping the *taa tucus,* and each day the owners would dance off at dawn to notify their guests. Even families who had gone downriver to work their gardens were visited, and the group could be heard for a long time as they bellowed and splashed down the Inuya. A couple of times they stayed to sing and dance overnight, but more often they returned to Varadero at dusk. Once they left late in the afternoon and returned at midnight, when the chanting men were reflected eerily in the inky waters of the river by the light of their flaming firebrands.

The routine was interrupted on the ninth day, when the men went out to cut firewood; on the tenth day to cut and hang some fifty stalks of bananas in one of the airstrip huts; and on the eleventh day to bring in the wood they had previously cut. It was a huge pile, probably a good half ton in all, and the men worked hard to chop it into kindling.

Most of the evening social events took place around Pansitimba's house or his uncle's house next door, and after the bananas were hung, snake lines of the whole singing, grunting, yelling troop hopped and shuffled the twenty yards to the banana house to check on the ripening stems.

During all these preliminaries only two women, the owners' wives, had regularly joined in with the men, and one of them had made sixteen very large pots for cooking up the banana brew. Finally, two nights before the ceremony proper, all guests, both near and far, were rounded up and assembled into one final snake line for the inspection tour of the now fully ripened fruit. After the usual night-long singing, the pots were carefully aligned inside the house, surrounded by kindling, and half filled with water. The plantains were then stripped from their stalks and piled into sixteen enormous heaps outside the house, where the men proceeded to skin them, bite off the soft outer flesh, and after a good chew spit the mouthful into temporary containers. In the meantime women mashed the hard leftover cores into a paste which, together with the masticated pulp, was transferred to the pots. When the vast piles of plantains had been reduced to a mess of empty skins, the

95

contents of the big pots were thoroughly stirred and strained, and the kindling was lighted. Bringing the contents to a boil was an unpleasant business: the fires smoked so heavily that at the end the men could only dash in, give a pot a quick stir with a paddle, and dash out again, coughing and sputtering the while. But finally the fires died down to embers, the pots steamed cheerfully, and the smoke dissipated enough for the first part of the ceremony proper to begin.

All the small children were gathered into a group. Then two men would seize a child and, after getting the father's permission, would hold the youngster by his hands and feet and swing him face down through the steam of a simmering pot—Act One of the magic to make them grow quickly.

The second and final act began the next morning at dawn and was surprisingly short, lasting no more than an hour. Everyone gathered at the hut and began to drink the banana concoction: the men sat on benches and served each other, while the women and children guzzled at each end of the house. Now the essential part of the ceremony came into action. A man, feeling himself ready to vomit, would call to a woman to rush her child out to the edge of the clearing, where he voided his stomach over it. Then he returned to tank up some more so that he could vomit again. This vomiting over children was the focus, the climax, to the thirty days of hard work they had all gone through, and it was over in an hour. The distant guests, instead of enjoying the usual endless chatter with their Varadero relatives, now dashed off in a hurry. They were anxious to take back their share of the remaining banana soup, for drinking the brew would neutralize the jinx that had fallen upon those family members who had not shown up for the ceremony.

The *xuki oma*, or maize festival, seems to follow the banana ceremony both in general outline as well as in many details. There is a preliminary period when the participants watch the corn ripen, after which it is harvested, dried, ground up, and finally boiled into a soup. The major difference appears in the final part of the ceremony: benedictions are not vomited upon the children; the men merely spit the soup over them. However, this variation may be due only to the fact that the two owners of the last feast were very shaky about the proper rituals, and they may have missed out on this detail.

Banana festival—banana stems strung up to ripen; a huge pile of wood, probably a good half ton; men chew the soft outer flesh to a pulp, spitting it into pots; singing, grunting, yelling, they hop and shuffle to the banana house. The climax of the banana festival: vomiting over children. To make him grow quickly, the child is swung through the steam from the banana brew; dancing involves but four figures, three steps, one beat.

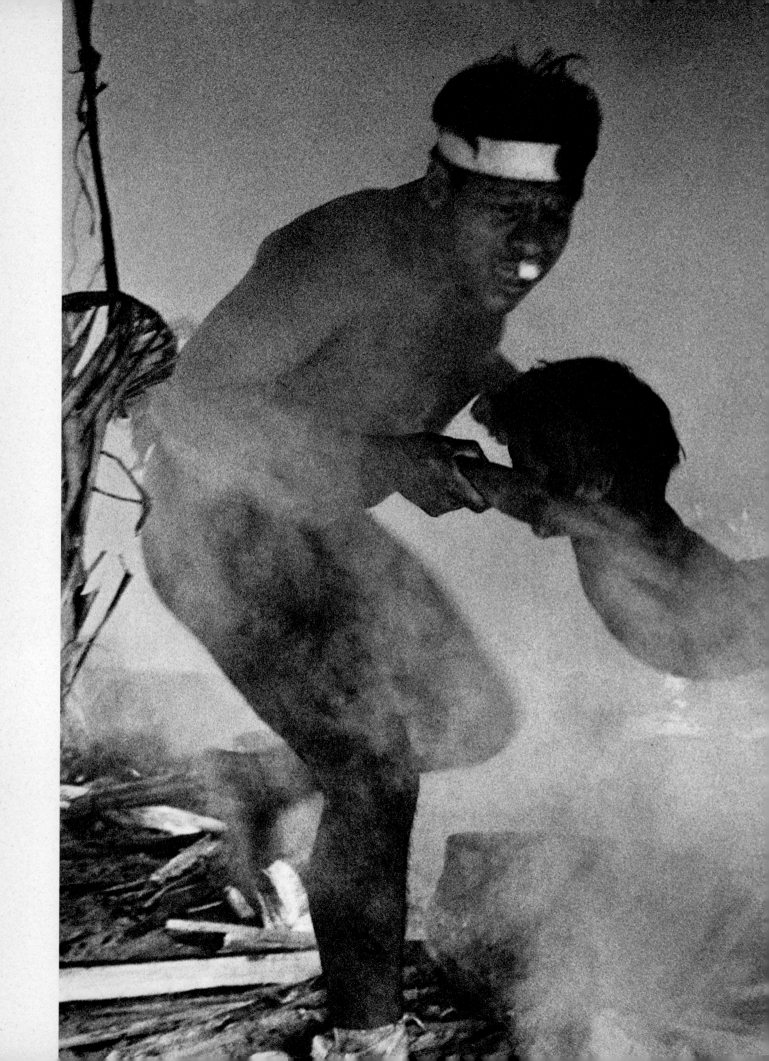

AYAHUASCA is a notorious and powerful hallucinogen made from one of three species of the genus *Banisteriopsis*, which grows wild over most of the Montaña. Cut into sections, pounded well, then boiled in water with or without other ingredients, the drug is used by nearly all of the Montaña Indians to produce visions. The normally staid *Handbook of South American Indians* likens these "delightful hallucinations" to those produced by hashish: "... all things appear to be huge and gloriously colored. There are visions of motley tinted snakes and of erotic experiences." Local whites, however, treat *ayahuasca* with a little more respect, calling it *soga de muerte*, the vine of death. The drug has recently come to the attention of some of the more fashionable American beats, who know it under the name of *yage*. William S. Burroughs writes about *ayahuasca* in the appendix on drug effects and drug addiction to his terrifying book, *Naked Lunch* (Grove Press, 1959):

> Yage ... is a hallucinating narcotic that produces a profound derangement of the senses. In overdose it is a convulsant poison.... Yage induces a state of conscious anesthesia, and is used in rites where the initiates must undergo a painful ordeal....
>
> Yage intoxication is in some respects similar to intoxication with hashish. In both ... there is a shift of viewpoint, an extension of consciousness beyond ordinary experience. But Yage produces a deeper derangement of the senses with actual hallucinations. Blue flashes in front of the eyes is peculiar to Yage intoxication....
>
> [Yage] is evidently not habit forming.... The Medicine Men who use it continuously in line of duty seem to enjoy normal health.
>
> [Some users] seem to regard it simply as another intoxicant like liquor. In other groups it has ritual use and significance.... All Medicine Men use it in their practice to foretell the future, locate lost or stolen objects, name the perpetrator of a crime, to diagnose and treat illness.

To the Amahuaca an *ayahuasca* evening is the most common social occasion with somewhat ceremonious overtones. While outwardly the *ayahuasca* binge has many of the earmarks of an endless cocktail party, its focus upon the supernatural world gives it a somewhat different flavor.

One of the protocols observed at Varadero is the restriction on the use of *ayahuasca* to men. Less rigid is the taboo that a participant should be sexually continent immediately before and after the session; continence is believed to prevent a violent stomach ache.

At Varadero *ayahuasca* is usually drunk as soon as it has been prepared. Within a very short time the drinker starts feeling dizzy, sometimes tinglingly numb, and is shaken by great gusts of trembling. As soon as an Amahuaca feels the drug acting, he starts chanting in a near falsetto, full of tremolos, the words barely intelligible. A man sings without regard to his neighbor's efforts, and key words are picked up and repeated by the others. *Ayahuasca* sessions frequently last from dusk to dawn, and the men sing virtually without interruption. It is an exhausting procedure, and the drinkers may not engage in another session for weeks, even months, at a time, though on rare occasions they will repeat the ceremony two, three, even four nights in a row. "It's not something we do every day," remarked Maxoopo, and indeed a number of the Amahuaca at Varadero have never taken *ayahuasca* because of the strain.

While it is clear that *ayahuasca* is used as a means of escaping from the humdrum of everyday life—and there are remarkably few peoples in this world who have not found some way for doing so—the Amahuaca consciously use the drug as a means of making contact with the supernatural—as a pipeline to the *yoshi*, the spirits, who are omnipresent in the Amahuaca's world and play an active role in their day-to-day lives.

As a group the *yoshi* are not well disposed toward people. Their ranks are made up of the souls of dead persons and of various animals and trees. They are viewed anthropomorphically by the Amahuaca, and when they are described the picture is essentially that of the Amahuaca themselves. *Yoshi* are both male and female, dressed in much the same fashion as the men and women at Varadero. These souls wander about the forest neither eating nor sleeping, though they may occasionally take up residence in an abandoned house. They have no personal names nor any form of social organization—no chiefs, tribes, clans.

Normally these spirits are seen only at night, in dreams. Such contacts, however, are relatively infrequent, brief, and usually unpleasant, since the *yoshi's* malign nature is uncontrolled: a man may wake up with a nosebleed from a struggle he had with the *yoshi* of his dream. And here lies the virtue of *ayahuasca*. Not merely do *yoshi* have a passion for the drug, but it turns them into friendly beasties, happy to join the party. They will appear by ones and twos, sometimes whole groups at a time, to sing and dance and talk the while, and when they leave, their place will be taken by others. In the course of an evening an *ayahuasca* drinker may chat with a considerable number of these mellowed gossipy *yoshi* who, being invisible and far traveled, know much of what is going on in the world.

While *yoshi* have superhuman attributes, they are neither worshiped nor propitiated in any way. No prayers or sacrifices are offered up to them, and should an animal having a *yoshi* happen to be killed, the hunter does not have to go through a ritual ablution as would a man from a totemistic tribe who killed a taboo animal.

In general, most animals that are feared or hated have *yoshi*. The most malevolent, most dangerous *yoshi* are those of the anaconda, electric eel, and carrion eagle. Less dangerous but still feared are the *yoshi* of puma, ocelot, cayman, porpoise, and rattlesnake. About the jaguar and boa constrictor, the Amahuaca are ambivalent. Only the king vulture is viewed as being usually well disposed toward people. However, there are some curious omissions: the two most poisonous snakes of the jungle, the bushmaster and the fer-de-lance, do not have *yoshi*; neither does the greatly hated vampire bat. And even odder, because it sets the Amahuaca apart from many of the rest of the Montaña Indians, is the exclusion of deer from the list—

nearly all the other tribes place them under a hunting taboo in the belief that they possess *yoshi* and become the living repositories of men's souls.

In the plant world only six or seven giants of the primary forest have *yoshi*, and only one of these, the *yoshi* of the *catahua* (*Hura crepitans*) is dangerous. This tree has a highly toxic and irritating sap which produces a painful itching and, should it get into the eyes, even temporary blindness, as many a woodsman has found to his cost. Otherwise the rest of the botanical and inanimate world is soulless: hills or rivers or heavenly bodies have no *yoshi*, nor do any of the food staples like maize or manioc.

An *ayahuasca* party is a social occasion. Anyone can drop in, for no antisocial feeling is involved in taking the drug, and women will sit about chatting while their men keen and shudder away. However, there are times when *ayahuasca* is used for nefarious ends; then a man will take it in the privacy of his house, summoning the *yoshi* to help him work his magic.

The most important *yoshi* connected with witchcraft is that of the jaguar. Properly conjured, the jaguar *yoshi* will tell everything the warlock wants to know, and will do the sorcerer's bidding, such as shooting an invisible arrow into the selected victim. If a man dreams that he has been shot by the jaguar *yoshi*, he will sicken and die. In most cases of sorcery involving *yoshi*, a human agent has dispatched them; luckily only a very few *yoshi*, like that of the maleficent carrion eagle, can work sorcery of their own. Only one class of *yoshi* is definitely not malevolent: the *xawakandiwo yoshi*. They are Amahuaca versions of incubi and succubi and appear unbidden in dreams to have sexual relations with the sleeper. Such visits are greatly enjoyed by the Amahuaca and, with very rare exceptions, have no ill effects. However, a woman sometimes becomes pregnant by a *xawakandiwo yoshi*, and the resultant offspring can always be identified because it is born with some impairment or deformity, a natural target for infanticide. One of Maxoopo's little nieces, who was born without ears, was allowed to live and is nicknamed "Yoshiwaku"—spirit child.

By no means is Amahuaca sorcery limited to invoking *yoshi*; indeed most of it is performed by the warlock using his own magical powers. A witch will project into the body of his intended victim various *yowuu*, as the ill-defined, evil-working powers are called. These *yowuu* are inherent in various animate or inanimate objects, and while they can be directed against people, they do not possess attributes of personality as do the *yoshi*. Maxoopo's father claims to have killed a number of people by such magic. He stirs up the *yowuu* by swallowing tobacco juice, and when the elementals are sufficiently aroused, he hurls them magically at his enemies, who sicken and die. Maxoopo's younger brother is also reported to have inherited much of this power, and both sorcerers and the Varadero community are convinced that the men have killed a number of people in this way.

It is curious that the Amahuaca, despite their belief that certain individuals have magical powers, have not invented the role of shaman or witch doctor.

This means that the magic they practice is nearly all black, while curative, or white, magic is rare indeed. Thus while the Amahuaca may project a magical disease thorn into a victim, they do not have a counter magic to extract it. In the other Montaña tribes a shaman is brought to the bedside of a sick person where, with incantations, dances, and *ayahuasca* visions, and especially by blowing vast clouds of tobacco smoke over the patient, the shaman draws the magic thorn to the surface of the patient's body, and finally sucks it out.

About the only preventive magic occasionally practiced by Amahuaca is an *ayahuasca* ceremony during which the *yoshi* is asked to help the sick person get well. However, the question of Amahuaca curative magic has not been fully explored, as the following curious incident makes clear. Pansitimba's grandfather was terribly mauled by a jaguar, and during the three days it took him to die, Pansitimba's mother was given some of his blood to drink. Now most of the explanations Russell got indicate that the potion was designed to help her father recover. But there were enough contrary opinions to becloud the issue: the woman was pregnant at the time, and the opposing view held that she drank the blood so that her fetus would grow big and strong and take on the characteristics of her father. Certainly no one else in the family who was gathered around the dying man's hammock drank any of his blood. So it is difficult to say whether this act should be viewed as therapeutic, as allied in some way to the Amahuaca practice of funerary cannibalism, or as part of a fertility magic.

In general the Amahuaca are quite thoroughly pragmatic in their differentiation between disease *qua* disease and disease caused by sorcery. The latter is only attributed to unexplainable illness—the disorder that lasts overlong and won't clear up—or to sickness that can be associated with a strained relationship. Thus a few days after Jawachiwayamba had finally eloped with Pacho, one of the little group that had been blackguarding him suffered a skin eruption. The man must have had some doubts about his position, since he was related to Jawachiwayamba and should have supported the marriage rather than oppose it. Since he could expect that his opposition would bring Jawachiwayamba's anger down upon him, it was natural to believe that the boils he was suffering had been conjured upon him.

This thoroughly practical way of viewing magic does not attribute evil intent operating through magical means to every untoward event: a hunter killed by his own arrow ricocheting off a branch had a hunting accident—no one put a spell on his weapon; an infant dying of diarrhea died from a disease, not from a magic thorn; if all of a woman's pots break while she is firing them, nobody cast a spell upon her—she just mixed too much sand with her clay. This pragmatic point of view is most unusual amongst the tribes of the Montaña, who normally blame such happenings upon the magic of enemies, personal or collective.

While the Amahuaca do not admit to a fear of death (such a revelation would brand them cowards), they do indeed fear it, whether for themselves or for others. Fear of sickness is manifest in their dismay over such minor disorders as diarrhea and colds—especially the latter, which spread like wildfire (since they have no natural immunity), and set everybody to hacking and sneezing most piteously. Serious sickness greatly alarms them, and being around a sick person makes the average Amahuaca most uneasy, for it is his experience that disease will usually strike many people in the same area. At times there have been veritable plague spots in the jungle. When many Amahuaca die of the same set of symptoms, their terrified relatives scatter to safer quarters, for there is little that an Amahuaca can do for a seriously sick person. He has no white magic (or very little), and his pharmacopoeia is limited to the treatment of minor disorders—the cuts and bites and scratches of everyday life. Death, then, is very close to the Amahuaca.

THE INFANT DAUGHTER OF YAMBA WACHI, Maxoopo's first wife, had fallen ill—from malaria perhaps—and one evening, distant wailing which kept on through the rest of the night awakened Trudie Dole and Bob Carneiro. The cries were still going on the next morning. When Bob and Trudie arrived at Maxoopo's clearing, they found Yamba Wachi in her hut, sitting hunched over the corpse of the infant. The woman was rocking back and forth in her despair, singing a litany for her dead child, the end of each phrase of her recitative trailing off in a loud, tremulous wail. The ethnologists were the first whites to witness an Amahuaca burial ceremony.

Yamba Wachi was recounting over and over again how she had given birth to the girl, how the infant had grown into a big fat baby, how finally she had pined away and died. With the exception of two small boys, everybody in the Varadero community had gathered to offer sympathy. "Yes," they chorused, "yes, the child fell sick. Yes, she died." And all the while Jawachiwayamba dug a hole in the center of her hut.

At first the hole was too small to take the two big new pots which were to become the coffin for the little corpse, and enlarging it was hard work, for there were many roots. But finally it was done, and Jawachiwayamba came up to the grieving mother with a few quiet words of sympathy. He looked closely at the bundle in her lap (for Yamba Wachi had wrapped the infant in a piece of old skirt), and then he gently took it from her, placed it upright in one of the pots he had slipped into the hole, and covered it with the second pot.

During this time the other adults made an occasional helpful remark to him. Their lowered voices, their serious attitude, and the deliberate care of all their actions clearly showed the mourners' sympathy for the bereaved mother. When Jawachiwayamba had filled in the hole, he turned to the group and asked, *"Canora?"* The gathering agreed quietly that yes, it had been properly done, and melted away by ones and twos, leaving Yamba Wachi, still wailing monotonously, to clear her house of everything that had come into contact with the child—rags, a pot or two, corncobs, the carrying sling. These were all put into a fire, and the ashes were thrown onto the dump heap behind the hut.

On the morning of the sixth day, the cremation took place and once again Jawachiwayamba was the undertaker. Recruiting four other men, he set two to splitting up Yamba Wachi's precious mortar, while the others were sent off to cut wood for the funeral pyre. With five big staves from the mortar as a base, he carefully laid the logs so that they formed a hollow in the center, and lit the fire with a match. (Fire drills have not been used since the Russells came to Varadero, an anachronism carefully noted by the ethnologists.) After the fire had caught, Jawachiwayamba went into Yamba Wachi's hut and opened the grave. A strong smell of putrefaction filled the air as the pots were uncovered, but despite the stench the woman claimed the "coffin," sitting on the ground to cradle it in her arms and wail over it.

The fire was blazing strongly now, and all the men, including Maxoopo (who had been casually sitting on a bench smoking his pipe during these preliminaries), joined the wailing woman in a tightly knit group, arms about each other's shoulders as they hunched over the remains. It was a long, tearful farewell before Jawachiwayamba broke it up to put the pots into the fire. Yamba Wachi was obviously reluctant to relinquish the stinking containers. Maxoopo up until now had seemed almost bored—it later came out that he didn't consider himself to be the father of the dead child, attributing paternity to his youngest brother. He now made what was obviously a ritual gesture by trying to wrest the remains from the funeral pyre, and the men, who clearly had been waiting for this move, put their arms out to restrain him. So, content to be dissuaded, he joined his wife close to the fire as she sobbed and chanted. More logs were carefully piled on, and the raging fire eventually drove the parents back—Yamba Wachi to her house to continue wailing, Maxoopo to his bench, where he returned to puff on his pipe and gossip with the men.

About an hour later Jawachiwayamba lifted off the top pot with a long pole. When some charred flesh was seen still adhering to the bones, the cover was replaced, and more logs were piled on. Then the fire tenders went off for a wash, for it was hot and smoky work. Another hour passed before the pots were opened once again. This time the fire had done its work, and the calcined bones gleamed whitely amongst the pale gray ashes. Maneuvering delicately with two poles, the men managed to bring the pot back to the house, where after a long wait for it to cool down, Yamba Wachi, still wailing loudly, sifted carefully through the ashes for the bones, which she put aside. The pot and its ashes went back into the grave in the center of the hut. She then swept up the burnt-out remains of the funeral pyre and carried them to the river where she disposed of them, handful by handful.

The following day Yamba Wachi had her hair cropped by her eldest son, after which she dyed her head a deep black with *huito*. But it was not until a week later, when the boy had finished making her a new mortar, that Yamba Wachi could complete the ceremony. She needed the mortar in order to grind the bones into a powder, and this she drank down in a bowl of maize soup. Then Yamba Wachi's whole attitude changed. She became once again her voluble and happy self; wailing ceased, the period of grief was over.

Ritual endocannibalism—the consumption of a family member's remains—is a common custom amongst many of the Montaña Indians, particularly the Panoans of the Ucayali Basin. Endocannibalism of the ashes of a corpse is not exclusively an Amahuaca trait. However it was once far more common to find Panoan tribes eating the flesh of the dead; some groups went so far as to kill their sick and aging rather than let them die before they ate them. Such practices are designed to banish a dead person's *yoshi,* and for many of these tribes it is clearly a disagreeable duty that has to be undertaken.

Many of the Panoan tribes gave another reason for the custom: they acquired the virtues and life force of the deceased by eating them. This was the most frequent argument given for exocannibalism (the eating of persons outside the family or tribe), and seems to have been almost invariably associated with warfare. In some tribes, it may even have been a major cause of war, with raiders seeking to capture live victims for the pot in order to acquire their prowess.

There have been a number of suggestions that cannibalism may have originated in protein-short areas, but this is an unlikely explanation for its occurrence amidst the bounteous jungles of the upper Amazon. Still another theory that the eater of human flesh becomes a quasi addict seems to receive some substantiation in the accounts of the early Spanish explorers, even though the addiction might only have been to the custom of cannibalism, rather than to the flesh itself.

Von Hagen, quoting Cieza de León, writes:

> ... any Spaniard who had the misfortune to fall alive to the enemy [the Quimbayas, an "indomitable people... hard to subdue" who lived in the Cauca Valley of what is the present-day Colombia] was, according to Cieza's observations, destined for the cooking pot. "These Indians are so given to eating of human flesh that they were known to seize women on the point of giving birth ... swiftly slit their belly with their knives ... and extract the child ... which they roast and eat." Prisoners, whether they were Spaniards or Indians, were never killed but placed "in a pen like a cage ... and well fed, and once they were fattened, they brought them out ... killed them with great cruelty, and ate them."

When the Amahuaca are asked specifically what a dead person's *yoshi* might do to them, they become evasive. One of them suggested that the *yoshi* would frighten them by shaking their hammock in the middle of the night.

The fear of death and of dying does not stem from a belief that an Amahuaca's *yoshi* might find itself in a hell or purgatory. To the contrary, their concept of afterlife is very simple and certainly not terrifying. The *yoshi* of a dead Amahuaca will wander around on Earth for a short while, until his relatives go

115

through the proper form of disposing of his body. After this the *yoshi* will go to heaven where life is led very much as it is upon Earth, except that it is more comfortable and less dangerous: game is ever plentiful, and there are no dangers from man, beast, or nature. Once in this heaven, an Amahuaca's *yoshi* may descend to visit his relatives on Earth; indeed, he may be summoned by them through the magic of *ayahuasca* to answer questions about other dead relatives or about relatives living far away. It is only during the first few days after an Amahuaca has died that his *yoshi* is in any way a possible source of danger to his kinsmen, and it is for this reason that the family of a dead person practices endocannibalism and goes through the elaborate burial ceremony.

An unsolved problem is why the Amahuaca temporarily inter, before cremation, only those who have died from disease. Thus when Pansitimba's grandfather died from the mauling he received from a jaguar, he was cremated directly the next day. So were the bodies of the murdered Ishman and his daughter. So, too, was the woman who was strangled to death by her husband's relatives when they found out she had poisoned her husband for the love of another man. But whatever their reasons, the Amahuaca have certainly developed what for them is an elaborate ceremony—a ceremony that appears to have its origins in one aspect of warfare magic seen in many of the other Montaña tribes.

THERE ARE MANY THINGS IN THE JUNGLE besides sickness that can kill an Amahuaca. Perhaps the most spectacular danger comes from the jaguar. Russell has reports of two women who were eaten in their upriver *chacras* by a jaguar, while at Varadero, Maxoopo's two wives were given an appalling scare when one of these large cats suddenly bounded into their clearing. It was frightened off by burning brands and the women's desperate cries for assistance—which their men, socializing down at the airfield, were most reluctant to answer.

There are a number of poisonous snakes in the area, and the bites of two of them are certain to be fatal: the dull gray-green fer-de-lance and the aggressive bushmaster, the largest poisonous snake of the New World. (A third, the handsome little red-and-black-banded coral snake, while possessing a virulent poison, is no great hazard; he is a shy and timid creature with a tiny mouth.) While infrequently met, these snakes have to be kept in mind as one goes through the jungle. Fatal accidents, too, have to be expected.

However, by far the most significant cause of death, apart from illness and accident, is murder: murder for lust, murder for vengeance, preventive murder, murder for jealousy, murder from irritation.

Some of the tensions and complications resulting from murder can be seen in the role that Maswanhno, an uncle of Pansitimba, played in a couple of such incidents. In the first example, a murder for lust, Maswanhno played the role of a murdering pimp. His half sister wanted to get rid of her husband because she was having an affair with her brother-in-law. Maswanhno removed the unfortunate obstacle by killing him while they were both enjoying an *ayahuasca* binge.

Maswanhno's role in another case of murder was a little more devious. This involved a half sister, Wocon (Maswanhno's father married three times), who married Maxoopo's younger brother, Ishman. It was apparently a most happy union, the two being devoted to each other, which created something of a problem, for Ishman already had two wives when he married Wocon. She died suddenly, and Ishman was brokenhearted. After a while he became suspicious about her death and became convinced that Cunan Wahi, his first wife's brother, had poisoned his love. So Ishman enlisted the help of his younger brother, Muxcaa Wundaa, and trekked over to where Cunan Wahi was living, about a day and a half away. They arrived at the clearing and found Cunan Wahi making arrows. Russell taped the following report of what happened:

"Is it you, Brother-in-law? Have you come? What have I done to deserve a visit from you? Come, sit down."

"I've been thinking about you recently, and so I've come for a visit," Ishman replied, as he sat down on the balsawood bench.

Next Muxcaa Wundaa approached and, after being greeted, sat down on the other side of Cunan Wahi.

The three men sat and sat, and then, all of a sudden, Ishman struck Cunan Wahi a hard blow on the head.

"Are you killing me, Brother-in-law?" Cunan Wahi asked. Again he was hit on the head, and when he attempted to flee, the two men began to shoot him with arrows. The younger of the brothers succeeded in driving an arrow into the victim's neck, just above the clavicle. Next, the two cut off the dying man's hands, after which they continued to shoot him with arrows until they were sure he was dead.

When the job was finished, Ishman spoke to Cunan Wahi's wife, Toshmo, aunt of the two brothers.

"Now I have killed Brother-in-law, with whom I grew up and with whom I once wanted to live. You are an old woman."

"I am your aunt, the sister of your father, and you have done me the evil of killing my husband, your cross-cousin."

"I didn't want to do it. He caused my wife to die, and I became angry. Being angry, I came to charge him with what he had done. And now I killed my brother-in-law. I used to enjoy being with him and his brother. You'll go to your older brother's clearing. I am going to sit here awhile."

Now Cunan Wahi was a Yaminahua, and thus a traditional enemy of the Amahuaca. His grandparents had come down from the headwaters of the Mapuya, one of the major tributaries of the Inuya, and the family had married into the Amahuaca. Nevertheless, Cunan Wahi still maintained relations with some of the Yaminahua and had befriended three men from that tribe who had followed his grandparents to the Inuya.

Here Maswanhno enters the picture. There had been bad blood between Maswanhno and Ishman, and the former feared that one day Ishman was going to repay him for some of the dirty tricks he had pulled. So when Maswanhno learned of Cunan Wahi's murder, he seized the opportunity to rid himself of a possible danger. Going down the Inuya, he contacted the three Yaminahua friends of the murdered man and told them the story. Their revenge was quick: they came upon Ishman in his clearing and shot him full of arrows and clubbed one of his daughters to death. The rest of the family escaped, though two were wounded in the process. (Ironically, one of the wounded recovered, only to become one of the very rare victims of a coral-snake bite.)

This, however, was not the end of the bloody story, for Ishman was eventually avenged by his younger brother, Tumonno, who, upon Ishman's death, had taken over the two surviving widows. Tumonno later managed to ambush the three Yaminahua, killing one of them. A grisly footnote has only just come to light: Ishman's first wife (Cunan Wahi's sister) had been very jealous of Wocon, the favorite, and today she can be heard very quietly saying that it was she who had poisoned Wocon, that Cunan Wahi had nothing to do with it.

Ishman's story offers a good illustration of murder for vengeance and retributory murder. Maswanhno's role as an informer adds an additional category: preventive murder. For though Maswanhno did not personally kill Ishman, his actions were certain to get Ishman killed, thus assuring his own safety. Such preventive murders are all too frequent, since many originate in *ayahuasca* delusions: the *yoshi* will report to a drinker that a (fancied) enemy is out to get him, which often leads the drinker to attempt to forestall this "threat" by eliminating the potential danger—through murder.

Murder from irritation sometimes occurs. While on the whole the Amahuaca treat their children most amiably, exerting very little physical discipline, they do sometimes lose their temper and thrash a child unmercifully. Maxoopo's four-year-old nephew cried so much that his enraged father beat him to death.

Body decoration takes on significance only when a man has murder on his mind; litany for a dead child; "and Sky fell down upon Earth which shuddered at the blow": storytelling around the fire.

II

IT IS CLEAR, as we look over the day-to-day life of the little group at Varadero, that the Amahuaca have undergone some profound changes. While some of these date from just before the turn of the century when they came into contact with the white man, the majority are the direct result of Russell's appearance amongst them. To an outside observer it is also clear that the Amahuaca are at a critical stage of their existence—the point of no return. Too many things have been happening to the families at Varadero for them ever to return to their original way of life—the life they led before the white man came. They have changed their social organization; they have changed the way they view the world around them and their relationship to it; and they have become acquainted with many of the material benefits which come from this enlarged new world.

Most immediately apparent, and certainly the most important, are the changes in the social organization of the little world that is Varadero. The settlement is becoming a village, with all that the term implies. The inhabitants are near to forming a community, with goals, aims, and desires in common, and with the elements of a set of social norms whose transgression will result in socially applied sanctions. If Varadero has not yet reached this stage, it will shortly, and Russell's facilitating role will have been crucial. While the term "village" implies a certain minimal, if not precisely definable, number of inhabitants, the present size alone of Varadero represents one of the great changes in the Amahuaca's way of life. This, too, is directly attributable to Russell; for in the memory of any Amahuaca, whether at Varadero or elsewhere, none has lived in any grouping larger than four families for more than three or four years at a stretch. Indeed, it can safely be said that no Amahuaca within the past two generations has lived in so large a settlement as that at Varadero today.

It is hard to say how big these groupings might have been before the white *caucheros*, the rubber gatherers, came into this area of the Great Forest. A number of Amahuaca have reported to the ethnologists (the Dole-Carneiro team) that once there existed three, perhaps even four "big" villages. Two were founded by the Rondowo, an Amahuaca subgroup, on the headwaters of the Purús: Maicha-huya near its source was soon abandoned in a short downstream move to Waxaya. Waxaya, in turn, was abandoned when the clan moved onto the upper reaches of the Sepahua where they established Xandia. If the first two sites are almost legend-ary ("My father's grandfather told this to my father, who told it to me . . ."), the third village, Xandia, is better documented for a number of reasons. Iriya, the Ron-dowo's *curaca* (chief) who founded it, is still alive and has had dealings with at least three white *patrones* who were rubber collectors. He is also reputed to have persuaded two other Amahuaca subgroups, the Isawo and the Shawo, to settle with the Rondowo at Xandia. The village is supposed to have consisted of some fifty huts.

But far more important than tracking down these quasi-legendary villages is an examination into some of the possible reasons they were abandoned; in what respect did the Amahuaca lose that social cement so necessary to the building of a viable community?

Internal dissension and strife is reported to have been the reason the two Purús River settlements were abandoned. What these tensions were we cer-tainly cannot say. But it is significant that the grandfather stories have it that five *curacas* governed simultaneously in these settlements, and the reports emphasize that the villagers "fought against one another." Just before 1880 the Amahuaca, then, were having problems in establishing a working village. Perhaps they might have succeeded, for the desire was clearly there, but their attempts were doomed to failure. They were suddenly confronted by the single most disruptive force in the Amazon Basin: the white man.

THE WHITE MAN came into the lives of the Amahuaca as the *cauchero*, and he came just at this critical period. By exerting almost continuous pressure, he effectively put a stop to village making. The depth of the penetration, and the intensity of the pressure upon the Amahuaca and other Indians of the area, varied with the fluctuations in the price of rubber, reaching a hideous peak in the two decades 1890 to 1910. Raids, murders, massacres, which were the order of the day throughout the length and breadth of the Amazon Basin, were equally to be found in the area around Varadero. There was no pretense to law and order outside the cities until after World War I. Sir Roger Casement had this to say in his official report to the Foreign Office on what conditions were like in the Amazon jungle some twelve hundred miles to the north of Varadero in 1910:

Indian-watching and white-watching, an elaborate non-stop soap opera; earning a machete by helping to maintain the airstrip; emergency dental service.

From first to last I met no authority of the Peruvian Government . . . the agents of the Peruvian Amazon [Rubber] Company . . . were in absolute control, not only of the persons and lives of the surrounding Indians but of all means of transport . . . of ingress or egress from that region [the upper Putumayo River] . . . a magistrate was said to be residing in one of the Company's trading stations . . . but I never heard him once referred to, and when peculiarly atrocious crimes were dragged to light, admitted and deplored, the criminal charged with them would be sitting at a table with us, and the members of the Company's [investigating] Commission and myself were appealed to give no indication of our disgust lest this man "might do worse things" to the Indians or provoke an impossible situation with the armed bandits under his orders. The apology for this extraordinary situation was that there was "no authority, no administration, no one to whom appeal could be made," and that Iquitos was 1,200 miles away. Every Chief of Section was a law unto himself, and many of [these] principal agents . . . were branded by the representatives of [the] Company in conversation with me as "murderers, pirates, and bandits."

This statement is an unconscious repetition of what Patiño Samudio had to say about the Inuya-Sepahua-Purús area a decade previously. This Peruvian, noting that a "roving colony of 3,000 [white] Peruvian, Brazilian, and other . . . workers" produced rubber "on a grand scale," went on to state:

In this colony, the strongest rules: rifles consecrate the laws and sanctify the crimes. . . . The power of the Government of Peru in these zones is not felt. Fiscarrald, Franchini, the Campa Venancio, and the Chinaman Francisco [two notorious rubber *patrones* and their hatchet men] are the sole owners of the Ucayali . . . and [its] rubber. . . . One can hardly believe that in so many years of exploitation of these [ever-] so rich regions of Peru that the Government has [yet to] send a customs agent, a governor, a soldier. . . .

Almost two complete generations of Indians were roiled and riven by the great rubber boom. Amahuaca territory, from the headwaters of the Yuruá River in the north to the Piedras in the south, formed but a fraction of the vast area set aflame by the white man's lust for the black gold—one vast, hellish stew of unmitigated greed and unalloyed barbarity. *Caucheros* and Indians alike were rent from their respective societies: tenant farmers from the drought-ridden Brazilian seaboard worked the rubber trails with the unemployed from the Peruvian oasis of Arequipa; whole tribes of Indians were kidnaped on the Napo and Putumayo rivers and set to paddling two thousand miles so that they might slave for their masters on the Urubamba, Tambo, Piedras, and Purús. This gigantic population shift was directed by conscienceless whites from England and America, Chile and Italy, Germany, Argentina, and the Levant, quite as much as by the Amazon Basin locals.

In this general turmoil the Amahuaca were not spared. One Amahuaca informant told the Dole-Carneiro team:

Caucheros would make *correrías* [raids or forays] against the Amahuaca. The Amahuaca made revenge raids. A man would say to his *curaca:* "I want to kill a *cauchero.*" The *curaca* would give his permission for a revenge raid. The Amahuaca did not work for the *caucheros* except a few on the Inuya, and more on the Sepahua. Instead, most of the Amahuaca killed *caucheros* and their families and stole what goods they could after they had killed [them].

These revenge raids are well substantiated by reports from the other side of the fence. Carlos Fry, the explorer and geographer, who journeyed through the region in the late eighteen-eighties, wrote in his diary:

> Liñan, laid out in his canoe [which was] paddled by Conibo [Indians], grounded at our beach at Cumaría one evening, having left his compound at the headwaters of the Tahuanía two days before; he was, as I have said, laid out on his pallet and wounded by arrows in three or four places. We rushed to give him what help place and first aid kit permitted; from him and his men we learnt that his companion, Vargas, had been killed by the Amahuaca of the Tahuanía because of the various indiscretions [*sic*] committed by Whites.

Even when the Amahuaca raids did not result in killings, they could be a considerable nuisance. Valdez Lozano, one of the lieutenants of the famous explorer-exploiter Carlos Fermín Fitzcarrald, wrote that in 1892:

> In the Tambo River the Campa Indians attacked me which resulted in three of my men being wounded.... [Joining forces with three notorious *patrones*] we paddled up the Urubamba and entered the Inuya River to make the portage to the Curiuja. [Here] we found [that] all of the canoes had been destroyed by the savage Amahuaca. We [thus] had to slosh downriver for eighteen days, our feet becoming raw flesh from the long walk in the water.

Such behavior brought its own rewards. In 1904 the Peruvian traveler Villanueva notes that the Amahuaca were:

> ...persecuted without pity by the *caucheros* whom [the Amahuaca] constantly rob and raid in their huts, stealing their firearms, their tools and their flour, without which it is impossible to exist in the middle of the jungle. In order to drive [the Amahuaca] away, [the *caucheros*] organize armed *correrías* from which the Indian always comes out second best, since if he is ever taken alive, he is dragged away and forced to work exactly as a slave, and is frequently sold as one.... To tell the truth, the principal object of these ignoble *correrías* is the capture of women and children in order, subsequently, to sell them at a good price.... The persecution to which they are subject keeps the [Amahuaca] ever on the move [so that] they have neither permanent houses nor *chacras* from which they can feed themselves. They are in a deplorable condition from this roving life. For this reason, their numbers are appreciably decreasing.

Sometimes these *correrías* became massacres. Here is another historical account told the Dole-Carneiro team by an Amahuaca:

> The Rondowo were very numerous once, but Peruvian soldiers killed many Amahuaca, especially Rondowo. They killed Estebán's brother. They killed 200 Rondowo. A *patrón* . . . sent for the soldiers. The *patrón* wanted the Amahuaca to work rubber, but they ran away. The *patrón* sent a Campa [Indian] *curaca* to try to get them back. He persuaded 200 Amahuaca men to return with their families. Then, lower on the Sepahua, they were captured by Peruvian soldiers. They tied the Amahuaca's hands behind them. They killed them with machine guns. One man

> escaped. He hid in a hole. Later he told the story to other Amahuaca. He
> died seven years ago. Estebán knows the story.... It happened when
> Estebán was a boy.

The ethnologists say that Feliciano, the narrator who was Estebán's son, could not remember the name of the *patrón* in question, except that he was "brother to Carlos." They suggested the notorious Matías Scharff, Carlos Scharff's brother, but the name didn't seem to register.

Such persecution, as Villanueva pointed out, kept the Indians on the move, and must be regarded as one of the major reasons why the Amahuaca attempts at establishing villages were defeated.

Yet raids of this nature were by no means unfamiliar to the Amahuaca. Ever since the Dominican explorer and evangelist Father Manuel Biedma first encountered them in 1686, Amahuaca history has been a story of defeat and despair. Their retreat from the Ucayali to the unnavigable headwaters of the tributaries of the Yuruá, Purús, Madre de Díos and Urubamba was the result of fleeing from their more powerful Indian neighbors—the Conibo, Shipibo, Piro, and Shetebo.

Thus, in the sixteen reports we have on the Amahuaca during the two hundred years that followed Father Biedma's discovery of them, only three fail to mention that they were the objects of great persecution. Certainly intertribal warfare existed all up and down the Ucayali Basin as it did practically throughout the Amazon Basin, but the unanimity with which the Amahuaca are described as being the victims of these raids, and never the aggressors, is significant. For with three exceptions the Amahuaca are viewed by whites as "docile, happy [people], easy to break in [to work]"; "very tranquil by nature [with] peaceful instincts"; "the inoffensive characters of these natives is proverbial"; "could be easily civilized ... as [is] shown by the speed with which prisoners, sold by their enemies, learn that which is taught them." Their Indian neighbors viewed them with scorn, calling them stupid, while the Piro nickname of *hipitineri* (meaning a capibara, a huge but timid rodent) has even gotten into the anthropological literature as a tribal name for the Amahuaca.

It took the great Antonio Raimondi—the nineteenth-century Italian immigrant who became Peru's geologist, geographer, voyager, and historian extraordinary—to look at one of the reasons behind these intertribal raids. Noting that the mission at Callaría, halfway up the Ucayali, was founded in 1859 by the Franciscans "with the object of preventing the frequent raids which the pagan [that is, wild] Shipibo and Conibo [make] upon the pacific Remo and Amahuaca Indians," he properly refutes the sugary fairy tale told by Father Dueñas that

> the [Amahuaca] prisoners who become [slaves of their neighbors] live
> most contentedly because they are treated with as much love and affection
> as if they were the children [of the victors, whose] daughters they marry,
> while in turn the captive women are joined in matrimony [with the
> raiders].

by reporting that the raids were made:

in order to steal the women and children.... They kill all the men . . . sell [the children] as slaves [and save the women] in order to slake their brutal passions.... This custom is due to [the fact] that all of the savages of the Ucayali [basin are] polygamous, and not having sufficient women in the tribe, the strongest and most vigorous rob . . . the weakest.

Reports of intertribal raiding are found almost to the end of the nineteenth century. While Carlos Fry, in the eighteen-forties, and Paul Marcoy, in the eighteen-sixties, merely offer hearsay evidence, both Father Sabate, in the eighteen-seventies, and Samanez Ocampo, in the eighties, actually saw these raiders on the warpath. Father Sabate wrote:

> . . . we spied in the distance an Armada, as it were, coming towards us; and upon [its reaching us] we could count 31 canoes which were paddled with dexterity by the many therein; they were the Cunibo Indians who were going to fight the Ipitineris [Amahuaca], and having this design . . . [were] well supplied with arrows, bows and clubs and whatever else they considered good for doing ill. [They were] travelling with rage and barbarous spite in order to wreak satisfactory vengeance upon . . . [these] enemies.

And Samanez Ocampo reported:

> Going downriver from Callaría, I encountered along the way two great parties of these [Conibo] who were going upriver.... Upon my return I again met them . . . there were more than fifty or sixty canoes [returning] from I know not what bloody tragedy . . . on the river Inuya.... The tribe which generally [suffers most from] these Conibo raids is the Amahuaca.

These pacific, even timid people were driven from their settlements along the riverbanks and lakes in the Ucayali Basin, and forced into the hidden depths of the Great Forest. The Amahuaca diaspora that occurred within the past three centuries transformed their original social organization (inadequate data hint that it was structured upon subgroups and organized by villages) into deeply suspicious, autarchic, single-family units—units quite independent of one another economically and only intermeshing at a few points in their social relationships. One of the results of their dispersion was a seeming inability to coalesce these individual family units into larger groups. It was as if they had forgotten the ingredients that go into the social cement needed to bind individuals into a community. In short, they had forgotten how to live together. Russell, when he came to Varadero in 1953, showed them how to do so.

Western technology comes to the Amahuaca; Russell is both teacher and missionary.

WHAT ARE SOME OF THE CHANGES that Russell put into motion, and how did he get them accepted? What does Russell expect to accomplish, and where might these changes lead? What, in essence, is primitive man's fate when he encounters a superior, technologically speaking, culture? For the Amahuaca have tasted of the white man's fruits and have found them good; their desire for the fruit will inevitably drive them from their presently inaccessible hiding place into contact with the Peruvian civilization of the Montaña.

Over the years Russell has brought into Varadero some of the most sophisticated, as well as some of the simplest, elements of Western technology, and he has brought them there through what is perhaps the single, most pervasive, most accepted symbol of this technology: the airplane. He has brought what we might, unthinkingly, call the simplest elements: fishhooks and nylon fishlines; the machete, knife, axheads, and nails; kerosene, match, and flashlight; tin can and unbreakable pot; shirt and skirt and shoe. If we look around Varadero, we can find almost hundreds of examples, each one, after its first miraculous appearance to a Stone Age man, accepted and taken for granted. More complex, because their operation is not so immediately apparent, is the gasoline engine which drives the water pump and powers the radio broadcasting and receiving set—the means by which Russell brings in all of the most sophisticated skills and information available to him from the S.I.L. base, including the medical advice transferred to the sick through the simple medicines and knowledgeable hands of a registered nurse, Russell's wife. And at even more complex levels one can cite Russell's introduction of the concept of the written word, of simple arithmetic, of strange visitors with stranger pursuits, of a morality that he not only preaches but visibly practices.

It is in the additive, collective, unemphatic yet pervasive influence of all these things that one suddenly realizes the extent to which the Amahuaca are experiencing change. And this despite the fact that on the surface their way of life differs not too greatly from what it was when Russell first appeared at Varadero a decade ago. And yet right now the most meaningful change has taken place, a change that only becomes obvious and astonishing in the light of the Amahuaca's previous history: the size and very existence of Varadero.

Varadero is Russell's creation. He is its founder. It exists today only through him, by his presence, and because of his principles and his motivation. The role that Russell and his family have played and are playing in this process of change must therefore be examined.

One of the most fruitful events in the relationship between Russell and the Amahuaca was his marriage in 1954, a year after he first met the tribe. Burtch, who had come down with malaria, was not able to return to Varadero (the Lingüísticos spend six months with the tribe and six months at the S.I.L. base or on home leave); and Russell took his bride of a month back with him. She was the first white woman they had ever seen, and her arrival created quite a stir. Russell writes:

It was rather difficult for Delores to adjust to the Indians being in our house all the time, sticking their fingers into food she was preparing, continually asking questions, wanting to try her glasses on, looking into her ears. The first house that Delores and I lived in did not have any partitions, and the people came and went at will, and so we had people staring at us most of the time, either from within the house or through the bamboo wall.

The marriage settled Russell's previously equivocal social status, since the adult male who remains a bachelor is in an odd position due to the sexual division of labor. Then, too, Dee had an entrée with the Amahuaca women that Russell felt that he could not, and should not, attempt as a single male. Her training as a nurse was also of great help in winning the confidence of the Amahuaca; and it stood her in good stead, for, as Russell noted, "it helped her adjust to having nude Indians around much of the time."

While Russell's social position ceased to be equivocal, his general intentions certainly were not understood. What, after all, was he doing there? What did he want of them?

RUSSELL'S APPROACH to the Amahuaca was and is of primary importance. He has never played favorites; indeed, he may be said to exude an air of disinterestedness, and it is probably this attitude that originally brought the people to settle near him. For the Amahuaca had never before encountered in outsiders such a lack of pressure, had never before felt that they were not being used. In all of their extraordinarily limited contacts with whites—in their occasional bouts as rubber collectors during World War II, or during very few and very brief stints as lumber *peones* downriver, or even in their women's relations with the army garrison—in these contacts, reinforced by hearsay about white behavior, they had always the feeling that they were being or would be cheated and abused. But here was Russell who didn't *want* anything from them: not their labor, nor their land, not their women. He asked only that he might stay near them. Indeed, his attitude permitted them to feel free to impose upon him, borrowing his ax or .22, or earning a machete, a flashlight, or some cloth by helping him maintain the airstrip or build a visitors' hut. Even Losano, the only rubber *patrón* whom they admit dealt fairly with them, was nothing like Russell. Losano wanted something from them, and even while the Amahuaca got quality goods in exchange for the rubber they brought him, even while they liked him and his shotguns and shells, his good cloth and needles and fishhooks, they resented that they had to work for him, and work hard. For with him (as with all the other whites) they felt they were conferring favors and being the losers thereby. With Russell, on the contrary, they feel as if they are receiving favors and are thus the gainers.

Such an attitude, of course, generates its own problems, and Russell has to walk a most tender line between Fairy-Godfather-*cum*-Relief-Agent and Billionnaire-Tightwad. To accept the former role would quickly render his life impossible. To become the latter would offend the social sensibilities of the Amahuaca. Yet the fact that he does represent the Amahuaca's only source of material goods must be considered as another and very powerful reason for settling at Varadero. Also, his ability to cut them off from this flow of benefits must be ever-present at the back of their minds. No wonder his words carry weight.

The settlement at Varadero grew slowly, very slowly, and it was a hard time for the Russells, not only physically, but also psychologically:

> Although I can honestly say that we did not expect trouble from the Amahuaca, we were not quite so confident [about] the Yaminahua who were said to have attacked the Amahuaca and the army post in time past. When there were no Amahuaca in the clearing with us, we would sometimes hear noises at night and wonder whether Indians were spying on us. [The soldiers occasionally heard] sounds and later found footprints and other evidence which convinced them that they were being visited at night by unfriendly Indians.

Russell writes that once while he was there the garrison "believed the Yaminahua were attacking and fired their rifles in the air to frighten them away."

Even today Russell has not quite shaken off his belief that a raid might occur, and his whole attitude is one of vast caution, almost of gloomy anticipation, which is reflected in the over-all psychological tone of Varadero. I remember well how different I found the atmosphere between my first visit at Varadero with the Dole-Carneiro team and the period, six months later, when I was a guest of the Russells. This, of course, may be due to a difference in familiarity with the language. While the ethnologists had a good working knowledge of Amahuaca, they certainly did not have the refined appreciation and understanding for nuances that Russell, an excellent linguist who has been studying the language for a decade, had acquired. Then, too, this was not their second home, as it is the Russells', and their involvement with and relationship to the families at Varadero was of a totally different order. But nevertheless, there was a difference: the community seemed somehow a little quieter, the people a little more tense perhaps, withdrawn certainly, than when I had first been there. One evening in particular stands out. Pansitimba's father came over and had a long talk with Russell. Before I went back to my new hut at the end of the airstrip, I was given one of Russell's rifles and a few shells and was told to douse my lights early. The Amahuaca, it appeared, were worried about a raid. It was a moonless night, misty, with the possibility of rain, and they were taking no chances; they, too, had doused their fires. The air was heavy with tension.

Luckily nothing happened. Nor has anything of this nature occurred during the decade the Russells have been at Varadero. Yet in a curious way, Russell's vague uneasiness—not about the Amahuaca, I hasten to say, but about their enemies—may have been transmitted to the families at Varadero. This in itself is an element in the force that is moving Varadero toward "community."

Russell must also contend with the hard physical grind of living in the jungle, and though he might have eased much of this burden by using S.I.L. supplies more extensively, he has deliberately chosen not to do so:

> The first few years I often went hunting with the Amahuaca men for various reasons: one was to prove that I didn't just sit around and look at a book and make marks on a piece of paper. [For] after I had learned more of the language, I heard one of the women saying: "He is not like our men. He doesn't go hunting. He doesn't fell trees. He just sits and looks at paper." [So I] determined to prove to them that I could do some of the things their men did. I learned to fell trees, although I still don't do too well at it. I began going hunting regularly and was very happy when on occasion I was able to . . . kill [animals with a .22] when the Indians were unable to hit the mark with bow and arrow.
>
> I have worked right along with the Indians in the construction of some of their houses . . . [in] making a clearing, planting things in the clearing, etc. I have done this in order to show friendship and to develop the feeling of participating with them, of being one of them in a sense, instead of separate from them. In the long run, this has paid off.

Dee's training as a nurse has also paid off. Not merely does she have a small stock of the basic drugs, but her nursing skills are backed up by the S.I.L. physician who runs the base hospital. Three times a week at a fixed time, the Lingüísticos in the field report in to the base by radio. Should they have a particular problem, they are given a specific radio appointment with the appropriate person at the base. Precedence, however, is given to matters medical, and a special time block is set aside for radio consultations with the base physician, who attempts a diagnosis and suggests the appropriate course of action (most of the fieldworkers are laymen without medical training).

The base hospital, too, is available in extraordinary cases. But here ground rules are quite strict. The case must be not only serious medically but also of exceptional importance to the community in which the Lingüístico is working. This is often a heartbreaking rule, but it must be followed since the hospital has but ten beds and S.I.L.'s financial resources are extremely limited (for example, it costs thirty dollars an hour to operate the smallest S.I.L. plane). Russell has been able to have a couple of Amahuaca hospitalized: Jawachiwayamba, a year before he married Pacho, had a large inguinal hernia which was not only unsightly but also might have strangulated at any moment. Since he was potentially a valuable member of the settlement, he was sent back for his operation.

The S.I.L. medical service (set up primarily to maintain Lingüísticos in the field) attempts to serve the tribes more by prevention than by treatment. Thus in recent measles and influenza epidemics (the mortality amongst Indian tribes who have never been exposed to these Western diseases is horrendous), emergency calls were sent out over the S.I.L. radio network to the United States, where the vaccine was located, donated, and flown into the affected tribes (amongst the measles sufferers were the Amahuaca) via Lima and the S.I.L. base.

Indirectly, too, tribes like the Amahuaca benefit from sophisticated medical science. When I was there in 1961, a group of American dentists descended upon the Montaña to make a study of primitive dentition. One member turned up at Varadero for a day and took dental impressions from Amahuaca volunteers, giving them emergency dental services in return.

When the Russells returned to Varadero from one of their earlier home leaves, they brought with them their first child, a girl, who had been born in the United States. The baby, too, seemed to draw tighter bonds of friendship between Indian and white, though, as Russell pointed out, "To have a small child in that environment presented some problems, for the Indians continually wanted to touch her, hold her, carry her about, and put their fingers in her mouth." Nevertheless the child did beautifully, but today Russell has a different problem: this daughter is getting to the age at which Amahuaca girls marry.

Despite the importance of the material benefits introduced by Russell, I do not believe that these are the essential ingredient in maintaining the settlement at Varadero. Rather they are merely desirable externals to the daily life. I believe the fundamental reason why this collection of families has managed to live together is that Russell has supplied them with the basic rule of communal life: "Do not kill thy neighbor." At least not arbitrarily, not out of whim nor as the fancy takes you. Should you insist upon killing your neighbor, do it only for well-defined, recognizable causes, so that he knows how not to offend you. For unless you establish such occasions, you won't have neighbors. Up until Russell arrived at Varadero, there had been no such ground rules amongst the Amahuaca.

This is probably the most difficult concept that Russell has had to present, and it seems to have been understood, for the twin facts remain that to date no murder has been committed in the Varadero settlement, and the settlement has existed for so long. These can only be explained by Russell's presence.

For Russell has been not merely a catalyst in these social reactions but one of the chief reagents. Lacking a social structure that includes the role of chief and shaman, the Amahuaca have indirectly, but quite obviously, thrust some of the attributes of these positions upon Russell. Advice is sought, often indirectly, and it is given, often as obliquely. And while Russell is a highly principled man, living to the letter of his Fundamentalist ethical code, he has inveighed only against breaking the sixth rule of the Decalogue (for he, too, recognizes that he would lose his neighbors if he were to attempt to change their way of life too rapidly). And even this principle he has gone about stating quietly, often indirectly, yet always clearly, so that the people know where he, Russell, stands. His influence can be seen in the case of the twin births, where infanticide would unquestionably have been committed had not Russell's disapproval been well known. The twins were kept alive primarily to please Russell, not because the family understood the basis for Russell's disapproval of infanticide. As he points out, "When we first became acquainted with the Amahuaca they did not seem to feel the smart of conscience over the strangling of their newborn infants."

143

This is not to say that Russell has not been attempting to get them to feel this "smart of conscience." As he says:

> We have taught the Amahuaca a number of things about human nature which seemed entirely new to them. The first of these is that man is not basically good, but is basically bad, alienated from the life of God and deprived by sin from fellowship with God. A number of the Amahuaca now seem to be convinced about their personal moral responsibility before God and men for their own actions. Some have learned that vengeance belongs to God, not to men. Some have learned that it is possible to love enemies. The necessity of repentance and trust in order for one to have fellowship with God as well as other basic facts of the Gospel, have been new to the Amahuaca, and we hope that some of these concepts have been absorbed by the people.

About twenty-five of the Amahuaca at Varadero have made "profession of faith in Christ," and every Sunday, which is kept as a day of rest, Russell leads them in a service. Not that Russell has any illusions about what this might mean to a number of them:

> [This] does not necessarily mean that they have been made alive in Christ. Some of them have apparently not been affected. They have just gone through the forms and have continued in their old ways of life. They haven't changed at all.

And as to the appeal that Christianity might have for the Amahuaca, Russell wryly points out:

> Perhaps people are superficially attracted by certain advantages they might gain in their particular culture due to becoming Christians.... Christianity is very different from their [the Amahuaca's] background.... Monotheism is something quite at variance to their legends and form of belief.

Those who have been truly affected, Russell concludes, are

> ... now looking to the Lord himself to help them in their daily activities instead of looking to magic formulas and other things to give them that assistance. For example, some of them now pray before going out hunting that the Lord will guide them concerning where they should go and give them success in using their bows and arrows. Some have prayed that the Lord would bless and cause their crops to grow, instead of looking to magic to do this for them.

THERE IS ONE ADDITIONAL MAJOR OBSTACLE

that has to be solved before Varadero can become a true community, and that is the "part-time" psychology of the settlement. For it is a part-time community, with inhabitants who are only part-time neighbors. The Russells spend only six months of the year there; the Amahuaca, who join the Russells during the dry season, disperse to their other *chacras* during the wet. And "disperse" is the correct word, for the distance, for example, from Maxoopo's downstream *chacra* to Pansi-timba's father's house is five and a half days' walk. Thus, to a large extent the old

144

centrifugal forces of their previous social anarchy are still partially present, and somehow they will have to be overcome before the group at Varadero can truly call itself a community. Nevertheless the people are acquiring a necessary sense of security—a feeling that they can live as close neighbors to people who are not brothers or fathers or uncles. What fears they now have stem from outside dangers: raids by their traditional enemies, the Yaminahua, or by Amahuaca scattered about the region with whom they may have a vendetta.*

Russell's vocation—his missionary activity—is inextricably bound up with the education and teaching of the Amahuaca. This is, of course, true for all of the Lingüísticos. However, Russell faces a particular set of problems common only to one or two other S.I.L. fieldworkers and their tribes: the problem of isolation. For few of the other Montaña tribes remain as isolated as the Amahuaca; nearly all are in some kind of contact with the Peruvian civilization of the main waterways. Thus Russell's difficulty is in part but one aspect of the larger social process of easing the entrance of the Amahuaca into a society with which they have virtually no contact, and of which they have no conception.

Essentially Russell must find a way of motivating his Amahuaca to undertake the painful process of becoming literate. While Russell's basic grammar of Amahuaca was completed some time ago, and while he has developed an orthography compatible with Spanish, the basic desire to be literate in either Amahuaca or Spanish is only sporadically evident.

Certainly the process is difficult for the Amahuaca to understand; not merely is the concept of reading and writing totally foreign, but their uses are only

* Russell, back from a visit to Varadero in the spring of 1964, reports a bloody footnote to the history of the settlement: In the previous winter, some thirteen Amahuaca men (seven of whom came from the Varadero settlement) went to visit a group of Yaminahua on the Purús river:

> Although the Yaminahua are [their] traditional enemies ... there had been friendly relations between this ... group and the Amahuaca.... As the curtain opened [a Yaminahua] jabbed an arrow into the side of ... one of the Amahuaca, ... and the audience knew that this was the ... final act. A [recently acquired] shotgun ... was used in killing [the Yaminahua]. Of the other four that were put to death, one was strangled with his own bow string, one was clubbed to death, one had his throat slit ... and one was drowned.... Even Coyaso [joined in, returning] with a six-year-old Yaminahua wife, after helping kill her father.

Three points might be made: First, that social solidarity amongst the Amahuaca seems to have set in—with a vengeance. The number of men involved alone would indicate a real community of action, a true ability to act in concert. Next, the Sixth Commandment seems not to apply to individuals living outside the Amahuaca's "community." Finally, the Dole-Carneiro team suggest that the murders may have been committed in error:

> Actually, it's very easy to visualize how the [event] may have occurred, [for] the Amahuaca have an intense horror of any [show] of violence. We obtained some sword-like weapons from them ... said [to be] used to finish off tapirs—and ... people. When Trudie [Dole] thrust one of these weapons toward one of the men ... to check [on] the way they were used ... [the] look of horror on his face ... indicated how close to the surface is their fear of hostility. It's possible that the Yaminahua was only jesting when he jabbed an arrow into the side of [the Amahuaca] since the [latter] always [have viewed] the Yaminahua as [a] cruder, more robust [people] than themselves. [But] the Amahuaca certainly didn't recognize [the] joke, ... killing before being killed.

dimly perceived. This is in sharp contrast to the other tribes of the Montaña which are in contact with the Peruvians. For they are most desperately keen to become literate, particularly in Spanish, for they view this as a major defense against the rapacity of the local *patrones* for whom they must work. Literacy is about the only way in which an Indian can protect himself from the local Peruvian bloodsucker, and only by being literate can he understand financial dealings with the *patrón*.

The Dole-Carneiro team turned up a classic example of this passionate desire to acquire what might be called "defensive literacy" on an island in the middle of the Ucayali. Here they discovered one Amahuaca family who, in order to send their boy to school, arranged to board him with the mother of their *patrón*, a lumberman. In exchange the boy's father was to fell one extra cedar tree a month to pay for board and keep, while the boy himself acted as a household servant during his free time from school. And to what purpose? So that the boy could teach his father how to scale a log, to assess the amount of board feet in it, and to check on the family's account with the *patrón*. Depending upon the time of year and the richness of the stands in the lumberman's concession, the Amahuaca father was committing between a tenth and a sixth of the family's income, quite apart from the value of the boy's housework for his board and room. But if the social facts of life are clearly understood by these Amahuaca in contact with whites, it is only feebly glimpsed by the isolated Amahuaca at Varadero.

In stating his hopes for the Amahuaca at Varadero, Russell has summed up his educational program as being designed to give them

> the education they need to prepare them for the contact they will have with outside civilization. This contact is inevitable, and we would be very happy if the Amahuaca could have a school and receive the benefits of sufficient education to enable them to make this encounter with the Spanish-speaking people . . . without becoming the lowest type of *peón*. Instead, we hope they will be able to take care of themselves during this transition and some day become worthy citizens of Peru, making their own contribution to the life of the nation.

The Russell children at Varadero: acculturation works both ways.

IT IS DIFFICULT for an American or a European to imagine with what disdain an Indian is viewed by the dominant element of Montaña society, and here I have carefully avoided using the term "white." For to be "white" in the Montaña is to be able to speak fluent Spanish, to write it a little, and to do simple arithmetic; to dress in Western clothes; to use at least a fire table (a waist-high, clay-covered surface large enough to carry a cooking fire at one end and a large clay oven at the other); and to eat only "Peruvian" foods. Indeed, because most of the "whites" or Peruvians of the Montaña have an Indian ancestor or two in their genetic make-up, the Peruvians despise the social, not the biological, characteristics of a man. Any man who can muster the proper forms can pass as a Peruvian.

To be treated as an Indian in the Montaña today is to find oneself cheated, lied to, and browbeaten in the cities. In the back-country river settlements and compounds the Indian finds himself the economic serf of his *patrón*—perhaps, though this is much rarer than it was a generation or even fifteen years ago, truly in a state of enslavement.

For slavery still exists in the Montaña. An article in the October 28, 1961, issue of *Expresso*, a Lima newspaper, headlined an "Investigation of the Case of the Child Slaves," and announced, "An investigation of kidnapped and enslaved children [discovered] on the plantations of the valley of La Convención will be the object of a rigorous official investigation." It went on to say that the Minister for Labor and Indian Affairs was to head an investigation of labor conditions on the coca, tea, and cacao plantations which sprawl on the eastern flanks of the Andes. It was but a two-column head over a four-inch story; so short a write-up, alas, was all the story deserved. For the truth of the matter is that no Peruvian reader could be overly surprised at these revelations. Slavery is common enough in the Peruvian jungle. Had I desired to acquire a slave while I was there it would have been neither very difficult nor very expensive to do so.

Slavery today in the river settlements and in the small towns of the Montaña is primarily, though by no means exclusively, child slavery, and child domestic slavery at that. For example, at Atalaya—the "county seat" and trading center for a very large area—domestic slaves were so common, so accepted, that five years ago a local Franciscan who fulminated against the practice had to be transferred for his own safety. While the temper of the town has changed since Father Holland Smith was appointed professor of metaphysics at the University of Trujillo in 1958, and the little slaves are today no longer so obvious, they still can be purchased at Atalaya. A word to a local Indian straw boss, together with a rifle and a box of shells, will produce a ten- or twelve-year-old girl as a "servant" or "maid." These children are purchased from their parents, and most of the girls become their owners' concubines as well as the household slavey. (Interestingly enough, while the girl remains but a chattel, the children of such unions are practically always recognized and reared with the father's legitimate offspring.)

Purchasing children from their parents in the cities and small towns of the Montaña probably represents the largest single source of supply today, but it is by no means the only way that the demand is met. Amongst the Campa Indians of the Upper Urubamba, for example, witchcraft has become the primary source of child slaves. In a case of mortal illness, the shaman will smell out the evil spirits involved, usually finding them in possession of a particular child. The child is thereupon thrashed senseless and left for dead. Many times, however, "civilized" Indians will come across the little bodies before the scavenger vultures can finish them off. After being nursed back to health, the child will either be retained as a slave in the Indian household of the "Good Samaritan," or sold to a local white.

Far more appalling, because it represents the tail end of a grisly trade that was once rampant throughout the vast length and breadth of the Amazon Basin, is the child acquired as the result of a slave raid. Though slave raiding has been mostly stamped out, enough of this traffic in human beings still occurs for one American, Ruth Harkness, to have reported as late as 1942 that:

> Cayetano [the village chief] was a notorious criminal whose ill-fame extended even to the Sierra. For Cayetano was a dealer in slaves.... Such was the demand that the Cayetano made frequent raids on outlying encampments, falling on them at night, massacring the adults and carrying off the children.... He made regular raids into the [Gran] Pajonal [an area due west of Atalaya] to capture children.... Some he sold to the *civilizados* of the Tambo district, and several he brought into Pangoa.... White people ... and all the civilized Indians owned them.

When she had leased a house in Pangoa on the Upper Urubamba, she found to her astonishment that her monthly rent of sixty-seven cents included the services of a "small slave, Lucho, who is very charming and useful." Lucho, she goes on, was the product of one of these slave raids and had been bought by her landlord for a machete and a length of cloth.

Slavery is only a part of the appalling legacy of centuries of exploitation that culminated in the horrors of the rubber boom.

Besides wiping out scores of tribes in the Amazon Basin and culturally murdering most of the survivors, the trade in rubber must also be held responsible for imprisoning the entire population of the area, white and Indian alike, in the "System." This hideous, closed circle of interacting social and economic forces has, like some vast intestinal obstruction, estopped any rational development of the Montaña and, indeed, of most of Latin America. The System embroils everyone and is compounded of varying proportions of dismal social and business ethics, unalloyed greed, and a vast and chronic shortage of money. In the System the Indian is cast as Caliban, hewer of wood and drawer of water; as the helot in this society; as the smallest link in an economic chain that stretches from the heart of the jungle

Patrón and *peones*. This *patrón* runs a whole tribe of Indians on a plantation; the company store; the floating peddlers. By and large the old ways of working Indians remain the same. Business is transacted over a glass of rum, or two, or three.

to the financial capitals and industrial cities of the West. The System, or at least a number of its aspects, is currently under intense attack, as is evident in the debates over the United States program, the Alliance for Progress. Whether any of the proposed therapies will be applied in time to save the patient from his constipation is highly questionable, for although the symptoms appear to be primarily economic in nature, they really require radical social as well as economic reforms.

The System operates on credit, but a type of credit far removed from England's "Never-Never Land" or America's "Fly Now—Pay Later." For the System is, to be blunt, usury. The System occurs wherever there is a great shortage of money: it is a nationwide (even continentwide) "Five-will-get-you-four" of the army and dockside loan sharks. With official bank-loan rates running around twenty-five per cent per annum, and the money difficult to get at that, it is no wonder that venture capital demands at least thirty per cent. The *patrones* of the Montaña, the men who deal directly with the Indians, are all too well aware of this interest rate, for they are themselves the victims of the System. Thus, most *patrones* are capitalized by big commercial firms, and both their grubstakes and the products they bring back, are heavily discounted by their sponsors. In the System the *patrón* does not merely collect jungle products, he also operates the local store— but with merchandise purchased on credit from the commercial houses.

I spent a couple of days with a *patrón* on one of the major tributaries of the Ucayali after my departure from Varadero. At this point we were some seven hundred and fifty miles from the Amazon proper and twenty-five hundred miles from the Atlantic, yet the Ucayali here is still a vast stream, some five hundred yards wide, fluctuating thirty feet between high and low waters. Despite its vast silt-laden bulk and an unbelievably tortuous channel, it is a fast-flowing river studded with shallows which, combined with a brisk four-knot current, makes the upriver haul expensive. Through much of its length it is navigable in a boat with a five-foot draft during the rainy season, and in a boat with a three-foot draft at all seasons. From Atalaya, Pucallpa, and Iquitos, the boats haul the gas and kerosene, the cloth and axes and machetes, the guns and shells and fishhooks, the rice and the rum, which form the stable stock in trade of a *patrón*. Señor X, with whom I stayed, is a man who has lived in this area for over thirty years, having originally come from Iquitos. He has a handsome wife in her late thirties and two children who are in boarding school in one of the nearby jungle cities. Señor X has "worked" the Piro of the area ever since 1935, moving his compound as "his" Indians periodically moved their settlement. A sallow, horse-faced man, he is a pleasant enough fellow to talk to, though voluble in his own praises on how well he has treated "his" Piro. He buys dried beans and peas and salted fish, a bit of cotton when there is enough to make a load, and sugar cane from which he makes a fearsome rum. Occasionally he will take in a bundle of puma and jaguar hides, but not alligator skins, for that market has collapsed. Lumber, which used to be his mainstay, he rarely touches. The current market is a tricky one, and many a lumber *patrón* has been put out of business through the imponderables of drought (flood waters are needed to float the logs out of the small tributaries); an increasing shortage of accessible timber stands; and the increasing difficulty of getting credit from the sawmills. The latter are currently in a bitter fight for survival: too many were established after the war.

Señor X, in turn, sells the Piro his trade goods. But, and this is the crux of the System, all of his transactions are ledger entries: money never, or practically never, changes hands between *patrón* and *peón*. The Indian is advanced his gun, shells, and tools; seeds, rice, and rum; and the totals are entered. Come harvest time, the produce he brings in is entered in a parallel column, and extraordinary would it be if ever his debits were canceled by his credits. Many an Indian has lived his entire lifetime in debt to his *patrón*, and until recently many areas of the Montaña saw to it that an Indian's children remained liable for their parent's obligations. A *patrón*, then, gets the Indian both coming and going. He sells on credit goods that are marked up anywhere from three to ten times the going market prices in the larger river towns; and he purchases the products of Indian labor which he not merely downgrades in terms of the going market standards, but which he frequently discounts for "transportation costs" or any other charges he can invent.

Señor X is full of reminiscences: when he first moved onto this stretch of the river in 1935, *correrías*—slave raids—were still made, and the Indians were sold off locally to other *patrones* and to the "city" folk of the river settlements. "Slavery," he says, "is still going on downriver (probably around Atalaya), but it doesn't happen here any more." And yet . . . and yet one wonders at the six young boys that are to be seen around his house. Orphans, he claims—orphans who were brought to him to be educated. "They go to school in the morning and work for me in the afternoons. I would let them leave if they had a good [that is, moral] person to go to—otherwise no." Advances in Indian living standards he attributes in large part to the rifles he sells them, "which eases their food problems"; to the free medicines he and the neighboring Catholic mission supply; and to the educational work of both religious and government agencies to which he contributes.

However, things are not quite as pretty as Señor X makes them out to be. This particular Piro settlement has been the focus of one of the earliest Lingüístico efforts in the Peruvian Montaña, and Señor X's stock is nonexistent with them: "He preys upon my Piro," says the responsible S.I.L. fieldworker, going nearly white with rage. She goes on to tell why the Piro have moved their settlement three times: they were attempts to evade Señor X. Dark doings are also hinted at: peculiar sexual proclivities; the habit of discussing business transactions with a *peón* only over a glass of rum (or two or three or four) in order to befuddle the Indian. Señor X is also accused of land-grabbing. The S.I.L. helped the Piro to file a claim to a section of land all their own where they would be free from outsiders. After a great many years of effort the Indians managed to get title to the land, when, to their dismay, they suddenly discovered that their section enclosed a piece of land that did not belong to them: it was Señor X's. He had quietly managed to stake a claim that put him, once again, right in their midst. While some fraction of these tales may perhaps be discounted as the bitter, righteous indignation of a nonsmoking, teetotaling, God-fearing lady Fundamentalist toward a Catholic who is more, shall we say, tolerant in his morals and private life, there nevertheless seems to be no question but that Señor X has indulged in some pretty sharp practices.

Many of the practices are not so much sharp as they are downright dishonest. Thus at Caballococha on the Amazon near the Peruvian-Brazilian border, the Ticuna work rubber for local *patrones*. Rubber in the early nineteen-fifties was being purchased in Iquitos, some two hundred and fifty miles upriver, at twelve soles the kilogram, while really good grades got fifteen. At Caballococha, however, rubber was credited to the Ticuna at four soles per kilo. A shotgun selling in Iquitos at retail for six hundred soles would be debited against a Ticuna's account at four thousand soles. The rubber equivalent of a shotgun was thus one thousand kilograms, a loading factor of twenty times the going market rate for the shotgun. Russell once looked over one *patrón's* account slips to his Indians and saw that the storekeeper had simply shifted the decimal point over one place to the right—a tenfold markup. As Casement noted a generation earlier, "The cheating of the men has been colossal and. . .deliberate."

And a 1923–1924 field study made by the United States Department of Commerce pointed out:

> An outstanding feature of the whole process is the importance played by the exchange of merchandise for rubber, the profits made on merchandise being at present much larger than . . . the eventual sale of the rubber. . . . In fact, the rubber industry over vast areas is sustained only by this source of profit . . . most of the [*patrones*] depend for profit more on the sale of merchandise to the [*caucheros*] than the rubber itself.

Though this statement was made at a time when the rubber industry in the Amazon Basin was reaching one of its lowest points, it would nevertheless hold true for both the peak of the rubber boom as well as today's lethargic rubber market.

The System, of course, requires that the *peón* buy all of his goods from, and sell all of his products to, his *patrón:* Villanueva wrote:

> These [*peones*] are truly slaves, subject to the *patrones'* yoke, without horizon nor future other than the limited view of the Montaña, to which their ill fortune brought them, and where death will surely come as the . . . final rest to a weary existence.

For woe betide the *cauchero*, whether white or Indian, who sold his products elsewhere, or who tried to flee from the clutches of his *patrón:* the only law that men like the notorious Scharff recognized was the *"Ley del .44"*—a grim reminder that the .44 carbine was the sole judge of matters in dispute.

This was not to say that men did not attempt to escape, according to Villanueva,

> . . . from the unscrupulousness or lack of conscience of the *patrón* who in every way exploits the wretched *cauchero*, his debtor: in the price and quality of merchandise which he provides; in the weight and price of

the product; even in . . . altering accounts at will. . . . So it is that a *peón* who goes out to tap rubber does not know when he will return, and there are [many] who leave for a year or two, yet only return six or eight years later, as I have seen those who have come back to the Ucayali, without a shirt to their back, and for rations but a little *farinha* [manioc flour] so rotten that the most disgusting of vermin would refuse to eat it.

Yet even when the law came to the Peruvian Montaña (which was not until well after the collapse of the rubber boom in 1912), it made little change in the life of the *peón*. For, outside of the few cities in the jungle, the *Ley del .44* continued to operate, even though it was not the *patrón* who held the carbine, but the Guardia Civil, a paramilitary group with a seventy-five-year record of exemplary efficiency.

As might be expected, the law was interpreted to maintain and support the System. Should a *peón* attempt to flee from his debts, the *patrón* would drop in on the local judge, who would in turn order the absconder arrested, thus unleashing the Guardia Civil. The Indian who survived his capture would be tried and jailed; the one who did not—well, it was only an Indian, and his death might well encourage the others to behave properly.

It should not be thought, however, that all this gravy reverts exclusively to Señor X and his fellow *patrones*. By no means, for he, too, is caught up in the System. In the days of the great rubber boom, there were at least four levels of middlemen who leeched onto the black gold that the *peón* so painfully extracted from the jungle: the *peón's* immediate straw boss, the *patrón* who supplied his necessities (on credit); the *aviador*, or roving factor-*cum*-trader, who supplied the *patrón's* merchandise (on credit) and who bought the rubber the *patrón* had collected from his *peones*; the wholesale house who supplied the *aviador* with the merchandise for the *patrones* (on credit) and who purchased the rubber that the *aviadores* brought back with them; and finally, the export firm which shipped the rubber overseas.

Today, the chain has by and large dropped the *aviador* link and the wholesale houses deal directly with the *patrones* (still on credit).

OF THE MANY INFLUENCES that are today moving in to change the life of the Montaña Indian, the greatest impact is made by the churches, both Catholic and Protestant. Only their influence—good, bad, but never indifferent—remains constant.

The Dominican Mission of El Rosario de Santa Rosa is at the confluence of the Sepahua and the Urubamba rivers, some fifty miles to the south of the Inuya. It operates in much the same way as the other Catholic Indian missions far from population centers, and attempts to be as self-supporting as possible; indeed the mission tries to produce revenue so that it can enlarge its services and perhaps even help the over-all work of the Order itself. To this end, it has set up a small sawmill with most of the lumber used by other Dominican missions downstream. In addition, the padres run a handsome and productive farm, with a kitchen garden, dairy and beef cattle, pigs, chickens, and ducks. After fifteen years of labor—the labor of Piro and whatever other Indians the Fathers could settle in their vicinity—the mission has become truly a showplace—if so distant a spot with so few visitors can be called that. The church, which can easily accommodate two hundred people, is flanked on either side by two large double-story buildings—quarters for the religious and dormitories for the Indian children. The original buildings are constructed of brick which the padres made from local clays fired in their own kiln; today, using a modern version of the rammed-earth technique, they are producing a hard dense brick about the size of a cinder block made from the same clay mixed with fractional amounts of cement.

At El Rosario three friars oversee an establishment that includes a mother superior, half a dozen teaching sisters, and one hundred or so children, ranging in age from six to around fourteen. The curriculum is both spiritual and practical. In addition to their catechism and primary schooling, the boys are taught handicrafts and a trade, the girls home economics and child care. One of the oddest sights in the Montaña is the children going to evening services. Here, in the center of a howling wilderness, street lights suddenly come on, an electric carillon starts playing, and the church, which has been dark except for flickering votive candles, is flooded with light from an array of fluorescent lamps around the altar. Two by two the children file in: first the boys in neat white shirts and khaki trousers, then the girls in bright cottons—the whole solemn crew a testament to the efficiency of the sewing classes.

I spent an evening with a bilingual Amahuaca at El Rosario and played for him a tape of news and gossip made by his relatives at Varadero; as I did so, the whole Dominican program came into focus. For the Amahuaca in his tattered trousers and his disintegrating shirt represented the Indian *peón* unhappily lost somewhere between his tribal mores and the dominant Peruvian culture. His children were becoming full Peruvians. They now spoke Spanish instead of Amahuaca, while their training in the mission's boarding school dissociated them from their father. The only place where these children could find themselves was in the Peruvian settlements. For them there was no return to the tribe: they had learned too much of white man's ways and had forgotten too much of Amahuaca ways. Thus, in essence, the Dominican mission is a factory for turning out Peruvians by destroying all things Indian.

Two and a half hours' flying time from El Rosario de Santa Rosa is the South American Indian Mission at Caco. If El Rosario is a factory for turning out Peruvians, Caco is designed to keep Indians Indian: to be sure, bathed Indians, Christianized Indians, clothed Indians, literate, Bible-reading Indians, but still Indians, not Peruvians. For Caco, like most Protestant missions in the Montaña, is based upon the concept of reservation: build a wall high enough around the compound, and the outside world will not get in to contaminate or influence the Indians who have been assembled there.

165

If at El Rosario the padres are wiping out the Indian's knowledge of his birthright in the process of transforming him into a Peruvian, at least they believe that the Indian can find a place in the dominant society: the new Peruvian is being "created" with all of the knowledge and all of the prejudices of the society he is being shaped to enter. But the tragedy of the Indian at Caco is not merely that he is being forced to give up his birthright, but he is being molded into an individual who has no place in the dominant culture around him. For there are exceedingly few places outside the compound where a Protestant can receive spiritual help; further, in the reservation, the Indian is given no training whatsoever to prepare him for contact with the culture of his nation.

For the reservation mentality views the world outside the reservation as either heathen and sinful, or heretical and sinful; life within the compound is designed to wipe out the former and protect the Indian from the latter. But like any animal reared within a totally sterile environment, a reservation Indian is sure to collapse when the protective walls of his artificial universe are breached, and the normal atmosphere of the outside world, with its germs and poisons, swirls about him. Never have good intentions produced a more certain road to ruin.

IT IS THEREFORE HEARTENING to see how a number of S.I.L. fieldworkers have attempted to strike a balance between the two poles of total Peruvianization and total withdrawal into a protected society. Much of this balance, I believe, stems from the fact that their educational and religious activities are organized on a linguistic basis—which is, essentially, a tribal denominator. As professional linguists, the S.I.L. fieldworkers are naturally loath to incorporate elements that would destroy their *raison d'être*—the tribe's language. Again, some have had the imagination to appreciate existing tribal organization and to put it to work for them. Pride of tribe and tribal culture is apparent at any meeting of S.I.L. fieldworkers.

Logically, the reservation concept should fit in naturally with this approach, but it has had to be rejected—in many cases simply because it is impossible to separate the tribe from the outside world. A number of Lingüísticos, for example, work with Indians who have long been settled upon land holdings of local *patrones;* most of their tribal culture has been lost, replaced by a pitiful copy of the Peruvian. In such circumstances the fieldworker is forced to act like a *patrón,* in order to incorporate social and economic assistance that is meaningful to both the *peón* and the local economy—for an Indian, after all, has to eat. The Lingüístico tries to encourage

Turning Indians into Peruvians: the Dominican Mission of El Rosario de Santa Rosa.

and reinforce what little tribal solidarity there exists, to knit the group together in a common psychological defense against the "outsiders." A few fieldworkers have developed quite sophisticated social and economic mechanisms which shore up the Indians' pride in their original tribal culture. Credit for a number of these ideas belongs to Dr. Efraín Morote Best, first director of the Government's bilingual educational program.

Two Lingüísticos have developed a marketing cooperative for the Aguaruna, probably the largest tribe in which the S.I.L. works. The cooperative is managed by a Government-S.I.L.-trained bilingual teacher. Twice a year this Aguaruna goes downriver to Iquitos, seven hundred long miles away, taking with him, on a balsa raft, all the wild rubber his fellow Aguaruna have collected during the previous six months. It is a long trip for a man to make, but once in Iquitos he can go the rounds of the great commercial houses to get the best deal. For while rubber prices are pegged by the Peruvian Government, merchandise in the commercial houses is not, and a shrewd shopper with a large order can substantially bring down the price of an item. Once he sells the load of rubber and allots each Aguaruna his proper share, the schoolteacher purchases the various items the tribesmen have commissioned him to bring back. Any unspent monies are deposited in the tribe's communal strong box in the *cauchero's* name.

A GEOGRAPHICALLY ISOLATED TRIBE has difficulty finding marketable products that can pay for transportation charges and buy the goods that are wanted so desperately. Obviously the ideal commodity is one that is in great demand. The Amarakaeri, who are almost as isolated as the Amahuaca, have found just the thing: gold.

The Amarakaeri live in a valley almost due east of Cuzco, on the Colorado River, an affluent of the Madre de Díos. Tucked away in a finger of jungle reaching into the vast wall of the Andes, they were essentially unknown to the ethnographic world until very recently, though they were well known locally. For the Amarakaeri, together with half a dozen other tribes, were collectively called *Mashco* (savage) by the Peruvians and were feared exceedingly for their fierceness. In 1957 two Lingüísticos managed to get invited to the tribe. There they found a group at about the same technological level as the Amahuaca, but socially far more developed, living in large communal houses, eighty-five or so to a house. The tribe is racked by endemic malaria, dysentery, pneumonia, intestinal parasites, and tuberculosis—while the white man's diseases—measles, whooping cough, smallpox, scarlet fever, occasionally brought in by a wandering tribesman—have decimated them time and time again. Today this group of some two hundred Amarakaeri have only three old people, lone survivors of an epidemic that killed off nearly all their peers two decades ago.

177

How were these Indians going to pay for at least part of the essential drugs they so desperately needed? Clearly their requirements were far beyond the economic resources of the S.I.L. It was equally apparent from the geographical location of the tribe and from the economics of transportation that the Amarakaeri, like the Amahuaca, had no exportable crop or product.

The problem was solved when gold was found in the Colorado River— gold that quickly transformed the Amarakaeri from essentially welfare cases into one of the wealthiest tribes in the Montaña. Actually it is not a remarkably rich find, but an energetic man, using a primitive panning technique, can make four to five dollars a day—really fabulous wealth for Indians, but hopefully not enough to attract whites (several are working the river in the watershed immediately north of the Amarakaeri with some, but not vast, success).

The Lingüísticos act as agents for the tribe. They weigh out the gold dust, estimate a man's probable earnings, and take his order; after returning to the S.I.L. base they sell the dust, fill the orders, and return with the goods in their next trip back to the tribe.

The rapidity with which the Amarakaeri have assimilated the material technology of the West is astonishing. The social consequences are equally interesting. The big communal houses are slowly being abandoned for individual huts, which is medically desirable because of tuberculosis. But the reason for giving up communal living is not so admirable: theft, or fear of it, has come into the tribe, and the Amarakaeri in their own houses are beginning to put their loot behind lock and key; the most precious items go into the small cardboard suitcases which every family uses as a strongbox. This wealth, which is so easily available that a family needs only to go on a little outing to pick up cash, is exerting a force that is, as it were, centrifugal: the tribe, already seriously dislocated without its elders, may well break apart the minute the Lingüísticos leave and the outside world comes in. For the Lingüísticos, unlike the Catholic missions, do not plan to remain indefinitely in the Montaña. When they go, who will market the gold and bring back the goods? The tribe would indeed be asking for trouble to do this through a *patrón*. Unless the Amarakaeri can develop the concept of collective action for the common good, it would be difficult to forecast much of a future for them.

The Amarakaeri Indians. Snufftaking is a cooperative affair; dressing up. Gold and the good life: making the pan; a day's work now and then will get all the things that gold dust will buy.

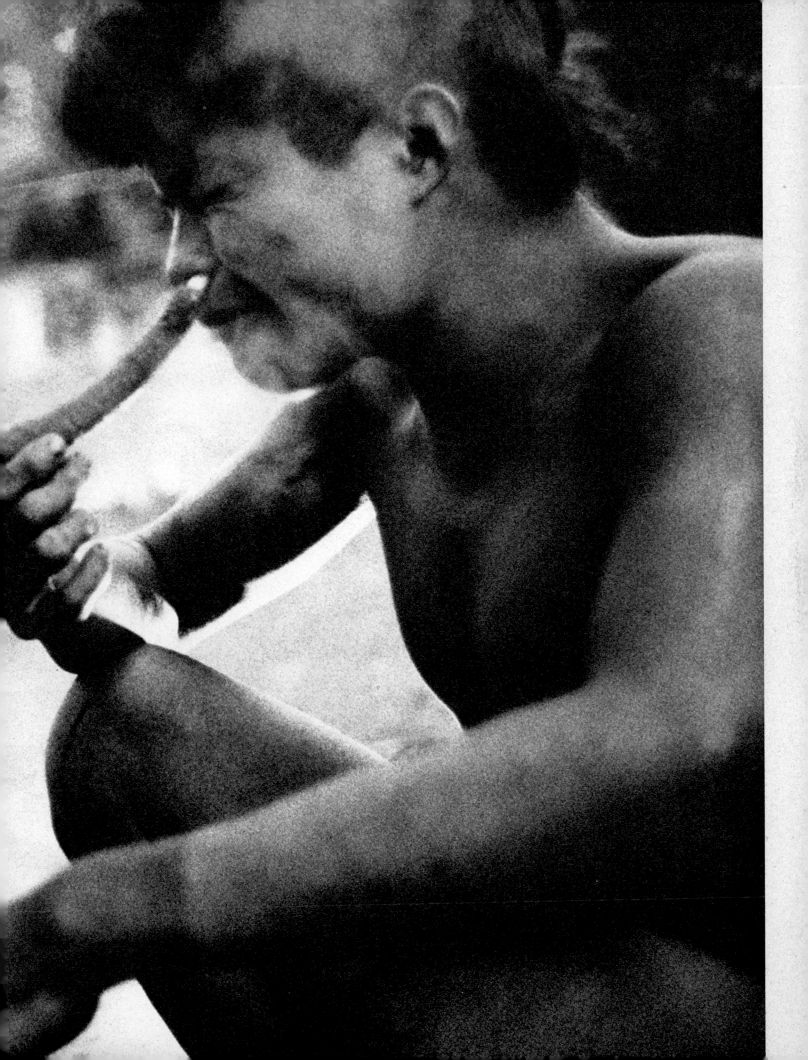

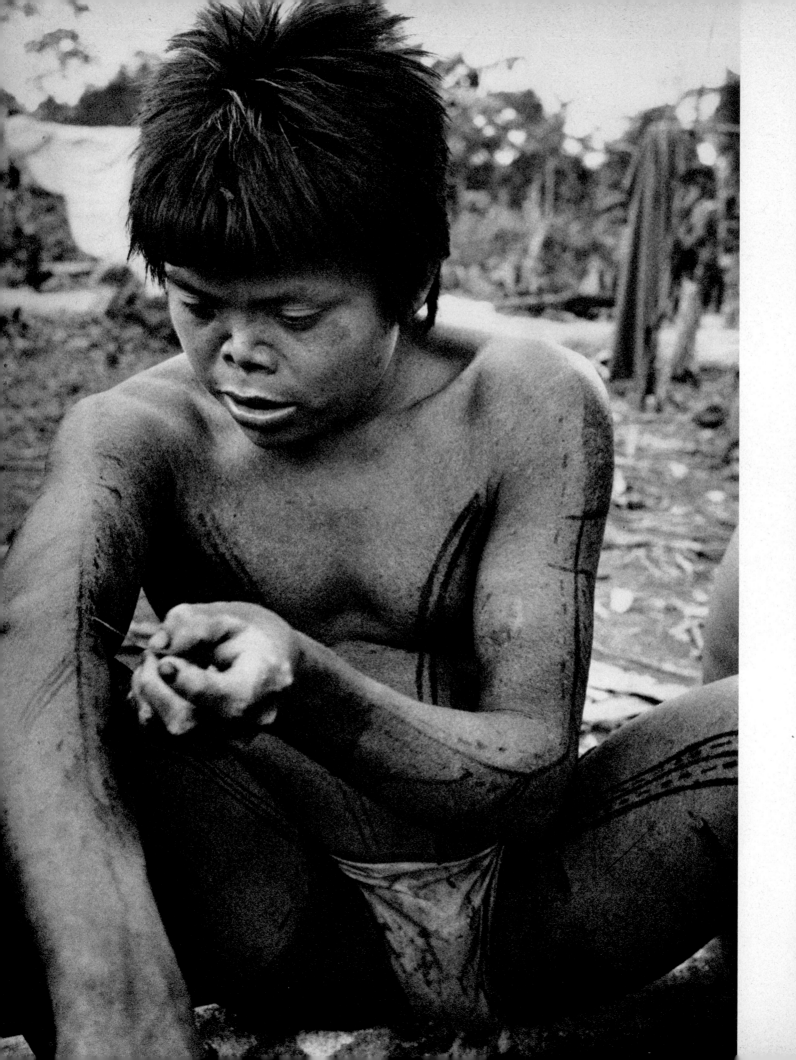

OF ALL THE TRIBES with whom the Lingüísticos work, the Ticuna, living on the Amazon forty-five miles from the Peruvian-Brazilian border, are probably the most sophisticated and the most acculturated. Like the Aguaruna, a number of their cultural elements lend themselves to the development of the cooperative idea, a fact noted immediately by S.I.L. worker Lambert Anderson when he arrived in Cushillococha in 1953.

Anderson found two mechanisms in the tribe's social and economic life through which the Ticuna's urgent and expressed desire to become Peruvianized could be fulfilled. The first was the Ticuna work party—a traditional call to neighbors for help. A man wanting to clear a *chacra* would issue an invitation to a work party, which his neighbors would answer. With rewards in the form of vast quantities of maize beer and foods, it was really a social occasion, and if there usually was less working than partying, the host was not particularly surprised. Anderson took advantage of the work-party concept and suggested that each individual donate a day's work for public service to the village as a community tithe; his idea found ready acceptance. Also, Anderson used the tribe's social organization of clans and clan councils to determine how this community labor should be employed. The result has been the total transformation of Cushillococha.

Anderson is also one of the very few Lingüísticos to recognize the tremendous importance of establishing community development projects on a firm economic basis. To this end, a village-owned, village-worked rubber plantation has been set out, using the excellent seedlings developed by the Peruvian Government's rubber nurseries (the result of one of the more successful programs of United States technical assistance to Peru), and the ten acres in rubber should bear within the next year or so. Jute, which the Ticuna have been growing at Anderson's suggestion, brought one man two hundred dollars for a three-month crop in 1962. Anderson is also investigating the possibility of growing teak. However, the tribe's staple market products are still manioc flour, dried fish, and wild rubber.

These products are usually marketed cooperatively through another of Anderson's inventions, and a most interesting device: the community village store. This store both buys and sells to the Ticuna, making a profit on both ends. The profits go into community improvements and into the salary of a full-time manager who is in charge of both the store and the cooperative. The manager will, for example, buy all of the manioc flour produced in the village, and he will travel with it down to Leticia on the Brazilian border, where he can get a better price than if he sold to the nearby town of Caballococha. There he buys goods cheaper than at Caballococha, and sells them out of the village store at a lower price. He is an extremely able businessman, missing few tricks, even picking up at a discount Brazilian or Colombian money, which he can use on his trips downriver.

With all these business activities the village needed a community boat, so in 1961 a work party made one large enough to mount an inboard motor—also community property. Today the Ticuna can go to Thursday market in Caballococha if they wish, or send their soccer team to local meets. As Anderson remarks, the boat "is one of the major additions to the village . . . it has been more than worth its while."

The neighboring town of Caballococha was one of the great centers of the rubber boom, having been something of a rival to Iquitos, two hundred and fifty miles to the west. When the Andersons arrived at Cushillococha (Anderson, like Russell, is married and is raising his family amongst the Ticuna), they found the people in "a typical state of indebtedness to the *patrones* of Caballococha." Anderson says, "One of the great holds that the *patrones* have over the Indians is their declaration that 'all the land you are working belongs to me, and therefore, the products are to be sold only to me.'" Morote Best, along with Anderson, went to work on their contacts in various ministries. Finally, the Ticuna's land around their lake was made into an official reservation by the Ministry of Agriculture, and the Indians were given exclusive rights over the area. This "resulted in friction with the *patrones*," recalls Anderson, "but since then they have pretty well forgotten it."

The Peruvian Government has a policy of developing frontier settlements both to assure a loyal and satisfied citizenry and to create showplaces that can be pointed to with patriotic pride. Recently it supported the Ticuna school system in an unusual way: with the gift of an electric generator, whose influence in educational matters should not be underrated. Anderson, whose mission, like that of all S.I.L. fieldworkers, is in part educational, remarks:

> The school has been making tremendous progress this year, 115 children enrolled in day school, and 90 adults enrolled in night school.... The lights have been superb for evening study, and they've also put through a village regulation whereby all children must be in off the streets and studying in the evenings. The fathers are paying good money for the lights in their homes, and they want to get the maximum use for their money.

The regulation Anderson refers to is a village ordinance, enacted by a mayor and corporation who were voted into office by secret ballot—this Ticuna village is the first Indian settlement in the Montaña to be recognized as a political entity. Besides the mayor and governing council, there is a registrar of births and deaths who is also the local *sanitario;* he was sent to the general hospital in Iquitos for a practical training course at community expense, and he will also work for a nursing degree at the S.I.L. base at Yarinacocha. This *sanitario* has developed a full register on every Ticuna at Cushillococha, listing the various disorders they have suffered and the immunizations they have received—mostly through the good offices of the

Cooperative elements in Ticuna culture—S.I.L. fieldworker Lambert Anderson has brought the tribe into Montaña society; the Peruvian Government has given the Ticuna an electric generator and title to their rich lands; products are marketed cooperatively in a communally made canoe; public services are supported by profits from the community store.

S.I.L. medical service and S.I.L. supporters. Today the Ticuna are immunized against whooping cough, yellow fever, polio, and tuberculosis. In addition, one of the young Ticuna has started on the long road to becoming a physician; he is already in his first year of high school (with support from an S.I.L. backer).

With the exception of the Lingüístico base, Cushillococha is probably the cleanest, healthiest, and best-educated settlement in the Montaña, regardless of size. It has managed to harness a vast outpouring of social energy, and it has done so wisely and with much forethought. As time goes on, and the Ticuna learn the lesson that Anderson is teaching them, his influence will become less and less pronounced. But today Cushillococha like Varadero, is very much the product of an energetic, able, and imaginative S.I.L. fieldworker.

Unfortunately not all the S.I.L. workers have Anderson's skills and broad interests, nor are all of the tribes as fortunate as the Ticuna in respect to geographical location, ability to produce economically valuable products, or possessing established tribal organizations that lend themselves to cooperative efforts.

However, life for these Ticuna may yet become complicated. Consider, for example, Anderson's recent suggestion that, in addition to the community rubber plantations, individuals set out their own plots of rubber trees. Inherent in this plan are the seeds of dissension: a man's desire to help himself competes directly with his desire to help his community. This conflict may well erode the present excellent cooperation between villagers for the welfare of the whole community. In such tribes as the Ticuna, who have a long history of white exploitation and who live cheek by jowl with whites, it might be much wiser to foster cooperative activities in every way possible.

The conflict between public and private interests is no theoretical issue. Even today the Ticuna's cooperative manager is asking for a raise. If he does not get one, he will undoubtedly set up his own store within the community. The possible consequences of such a move may be seen in a tribe settled on one of the Montaña affluents to the Amazon. This area probably suffered more than any other at the hands of white men; it was infamous for the cruelty of its *patrones* during the great rubber boom, and it is today still very much in their grip. The Lingüístico in this area was faced with a tough old-timer, a *patrón* who had brought "his" Indians from another river when the boom collapsed, and who considered that any trade passing his establishment on the river was his absolute monopoly. It took over ten years of concerted effort and exhortation on the part of the Lingüístico to get the Indians to keep accounts on a cash-and-carry basis, even to assisting the son of a petty chief to set up and stock a community store in order to bypass the *patrón* and thus break his power. However, one of the first things the Indian storekeeper did was to open "credit" accounts for his fellow tribesmen, and very soon the people found their treatment by the storekeeper almost indistinguishable from that of the old *patrón* whom they had hated so passionately. But now the new *patrón* is one of them, and tribal loyalties make it far more difficult to arouse concerted action against him. The Indian who identifies with the dominant culture risks becoming a caricature of those he emulates.

THE VASTLY PROMISING TICUNA EXPERIMENT

shows how great an impact a Lingüístico can have upon a primitive society. In Anderson's case, his influence has been reinforced, first, by his continuing emphasis upon the tribe's economic development while pursuing S.I.L.'s religious and educational goals. Second, and probably as important, his long residence amongst the Ticuna has developed into an intimate day-to-day collaboration in seeking solutions to community problems and in teaching the tribe how to become part of Montaña society.

At a very great disadvantage is the tribe that does not have a cultural intermediary in residence. This situation is exemplified by the Campa village of Matoveni whose eighty inhabitants live in a humid, insect-ridden place on the river Tambo. Matoveni is on the distant fringes of the Montaña's civilization, which exerts its dominion only three times a year: twice through the visitations of the Government's malaria control crew, and once when the superintendent inspects the village's bilingual school. Matoveni's only significant contact with the outside world comes during one of the irregular visits made by a Lingüístico in support of its teacher, Santos C, a Campa Indian. The product of three Protestant missionary schools, as well as the Government-S.I.L. bilingual teacher-training program, Santos is both educator and missionary. He is also a man with a vision. Santos sees the village of Matoveni as a jungle town like Atalaya, perhaps even like the bustling city of Pucallpa, with an airfield, a hospital, and coffee and cocoa plantations; with herds of cattle and lots of people in proper clothes and shoes; a city where every man, woman, and child has found God.

It is a grand vision, but unfortunately not a practical one, for there is little, if any, foundation on which to base it. Matoveni is part of a howling wilderness, a wilderness which will remain one for many a lifetime unless it receives intensive, continuous, carefully planned technical assistance. But this is most unlikely to occur: the Government cannot supply it, and the S.I.L. is equally short of trained fieldworkers and the resources to maintain them. One can thus anticipate that Santos will become vastly disillusioned. Somehow, ways must be found to help the teacher place his dreams within the context of reality. For if Santos is not let down gently, the S.I.L. will have to contend not merely with an individual's anguish, but also with the reactions of a disenchanted leader.

Santos, a Campa Indian bilingual teacher who works for the Government, is both missionary and visionary; Will Kindberg, S.I.L. fieldworker.

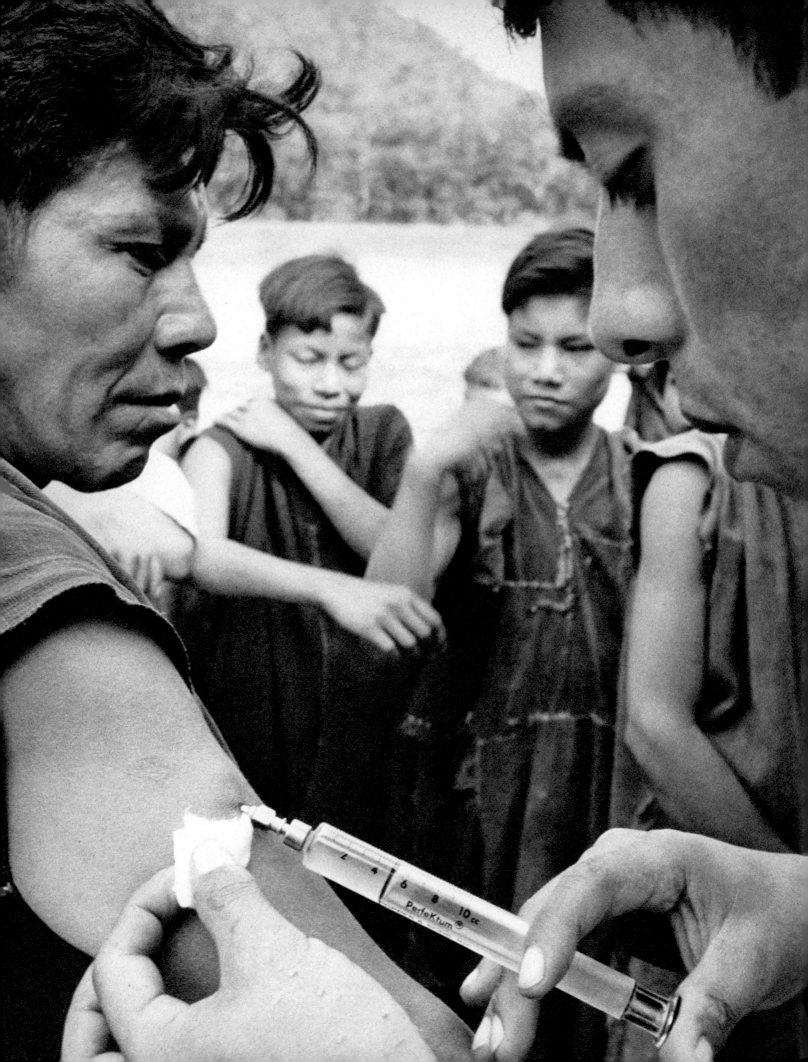

THE RAPACITY OF THE PATRONES has become somewhat moderated during the past couple of decades by the changes that have taken place in the social climate of the Montaña's two big cities, the great Amazon port of Iquitos and the newer jungle city, Pucallpa. They have speeded up the transition of the Indian from slavery to independent status, through a variety of mechanisms.

While the law first came into the Montaña as a process of adjudicating clashes between the big rubber operators at the turn of the century, it gradually seeped down to all strata of society, finally reaching the Indian when the collapse of the rubber boom removed the catastrophic pressure for his labor. The replacement of the barter-*cum*-credit system by the cash transaction benefited the Indian day laborer by forcing him to learn the economic facts of life out of self-preservation. The city also plays a vital role in helping the Indian become a "Peruvian" through the anonymity it offers him during the process of detribalization. He learns pidgin Spanish and the rudiments of arithmetic, and he is given concrete examples of the white man's morals, mores, dress, food as examples to ape. Broad conformity to the white man's norms is all that is asked of the Indian, and their acquisition is often actively encouraged in the city—for example, getting his children into school.

Iquitos is a wildly improbable town, with wildly improbable beginnings. A century ago it was nothing but an Indian village of thirty huts, four hundred souls—and naked, miserable souls at that. Yet a generation later the rubber boom had multiplied the figure a hundredfold, and Iquitos had become a city with electricity and champagne but no running water; a city with a steel clubhouse made by the famous Eiffel of the Tower, but no sewers. Then came the bust, with three and a half decades of stagnation. Today Iquitos is booming once again. There are traffic jams on paved streets that lead to nowhere, and the handsome tile and stucco buildings of the first boom are being excoriated by the neon signs of the second. A new brick residential section, built within the past decade, is flanked on the landward side by an older suburb of neat thatched clapboard and bamboo houses nestling amidst a checkerboard of noisome open sewers, while in the lee of the river bend bob a myriad balsa barges, the newest additions to the floating slums of the detribalized Indians. Iquitos boasts such resources as the best landing field between Quito and Rio, a five-hundred-bed hospital, and the biggest sawmill in South America. Yet it is a city that still uses a man's back to move the jungle's products an agonizing hundred feet from riverboat to warehouse. In the glitter of its shops and movie houses, in the vast variety of goods and services, in the fact that it is the administrative center (both civil and military) of the area, Iquitos shows that it is, indeed, the capital city of the Montaña. Yet it is not really part of the main current of Peruvian life: the strangling jungle and the impassable Andes force Iquitos to look to the industrial nations bordering the Atlantic, rather than to Lima.

It is just because of these geographical realities that Iquitos may eventually be forced to take second place to Pucallpa and the other river towns closer to the great mountain barrier. Pucallpa is a graphic lesson in the economics of communication and the radical transformation of an area. In 1915 three small compounds were established at Pucallpa, but by 1922, according to a river captain's report, all had disappeared; in 1926 traders considered the area to be one of the poorest and most backward of the central Montaña. By 1932 things were beginning to look up: Pucallpa was made a military aviation stop, and the traffic brought new business to the village. Slowly it grew, reaching a population of some two thousand in 1940.

Then, in 1943, after enormous difficulties, a road was brought from Lima through the Andes into Pucallpa—and what a road it is. Starting in a desert where total annual rainfall is measured in hundredths of an inch, the road ends in a jungle where one meteorological station regularly records one hundred and ninety inches per year. Twice it crosses the Andes on passes over fifteen thousand feet (one scratches sixteen thousand). It is nicely paved and two cars wide for nearly the first half of its length, but the last part (which is now also being paved) is gravel or mud, the latter so slick, so soft when wet, that the road is closed after every rain; and so narrow on the eastern face of the Andes that traffic drives only in one direction, depending on the day of the week. Yet despite the landslides that block it with disheartening frequency, despite the axle-deep mud after every rain, despite the fantastically high trucking costs, the road has transformed Pucallpa.

In the twenty years since the road was opened, Pucallpa has grown into a bustling town of about thirty thousand people. And for the first time the wealth of the jungle is reaching Peru's economic centers in appreciable quantities, rather than being shipped via the Amazon to Europe and North America. Pucallpa has none of the charm of Iquitos and is far less a "city." There has, for example, been no attempt at municipal improvements. Outside of half a dozen blocks of stuccoed brick houses, hotels, and business establishments, the town is essentially composed of frame huts; only two blocks—the business district—are paved; elsewhere the red clay becomes one vast sea of mud after a rain.

Pucallpa is a raw town, full of life and noise: the braying of the water vendors' mules, the howling radios, the squeals of the pigs rooting in the road. Raw sewage flows through open sewers; at every other corner in the downtown section, dim electric lights flicker from posts that lean drunkenly. In the commercial establishments customers forage through huge piles of merchandise from the four corners of the world. Everywhere there is a profusion of the shoddy, the garish; and everywhere there is an elaboration of bills of lading, ledger entries, stamped

Pucallpa: A floating slum. Raw sewage flows down to the Ucayali River; the vast log rafts represent Pucallpa's major product, lumber; the glitter of the city gives the Indian a concrete example of the white man's ways; the Army helps mold Indians into Peruvians.

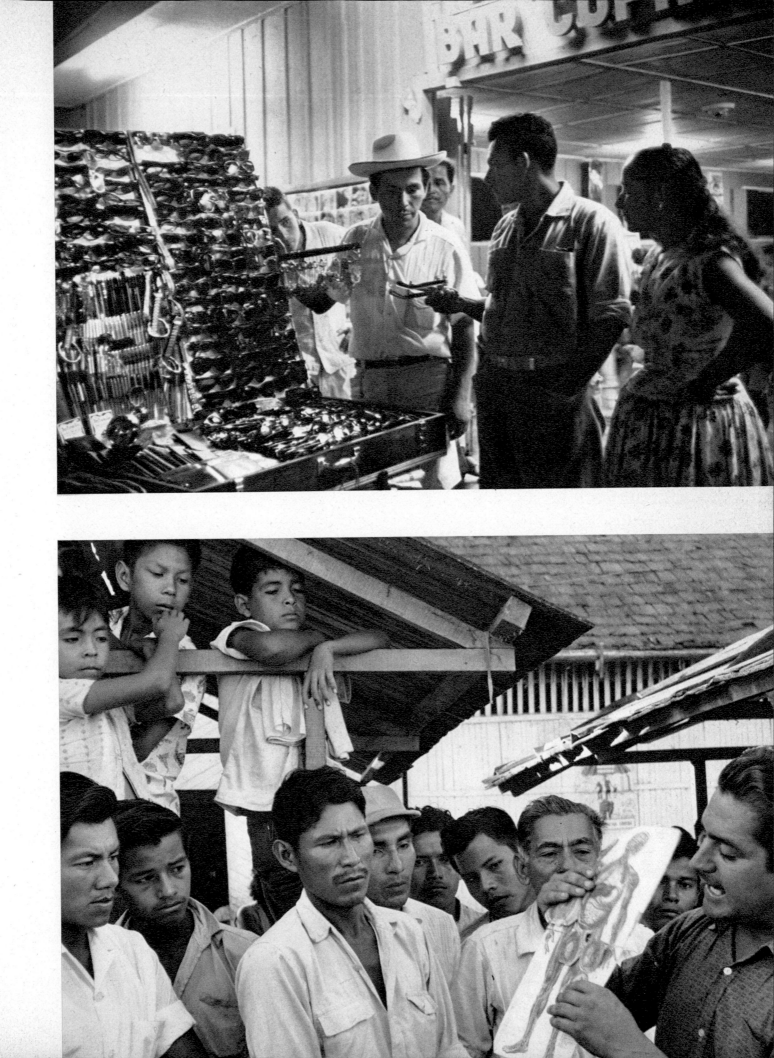

legal paper, each floridly attesting that so-and-so bought and paid for his purchases. All day and late into the night, wrecks of buses jolt heavily from one vast rut to another grinding their way to peripheral settlements three and four miles out of the city. And always, hanging around the lumber trucks—for lumber is Pucallpa's major product—would-be travelers are bargaining their way to points along the road to Lima. Down by the Ucayali, perhaps three quarters of a mile wide here, the same scene has innumerable variations: Who can haul a canoe behind his *peque-peque* (motorboat)? Who will tug a raft of cut lumber downriver? And everywhere are logs: logs littering the mud beach, logs in vast rafts tethered in quiet bays; logs slithering massively up the riverbanks, pulled by flailing wire ropes into the maws of sawmills.

Through all this din and activity stalk uniforms: officials of the port command, the forestry service, the military, the police, the Guardia Civil, pilots and crews of airplanes—everyone inscrutable behind dark glasses (as a status symbol they are on the way out: cheap plastic sunglasses are peddled on every street corner). Yet the uniforms are but gaudy raisins in the doughy mass of population: the men wear faded khakis, the women dreary ginghams; only the fancy palmetto hats, shiny boots, and bristling mustaches distinguish *patrón* from *peón*.

Pucallpa, too, has its slums. As in Iquitos, there are the floating single-roomed thatched huts built upon balsa log rafts. But here the population is truly floating, arriving on the beach for two, three, four months at a time, and then vanishing. The permanent slum population raises its huts on stilts just below high-water mark, and under the ten-foot poles a happy menagerie of pigs, chickens, dogs, and children play hide-and-seek all day. Most of these slum dwellers are detribalized Indians well along the road to becoming assimilated as Peruvians. Mostly illiterate (though their children are going to school), they speak a bastard Spanish, with a vocabulary of perhaps fifteen hundred words. Their Peruvian diet, consisting primarily of fish, manioc flour, and bananas (for they have cleared *chacras* across the river), is beggarly in both range and balance compared with their original tribal diet. They are clothed in rags and tatters of European dress and eke out the barest of existences as day laborers, trying to maintain a family on approximately sixty cents a day. They are not a healthy group: infant mortality is around fifty per cent, largely from whooping cough and the fact that over two thirds of the births are not attended by trained midwives; tuberculosis and the venereal diseases are almost endemic—the latter almost pandemic, due to the truly heroic efforts of amorous truckdrivers and to the desperate need of the women to augment the family income by a few extra cents. Leprosy, too, is coming into the area. Though still rare here in contrast to the eastern Amazon reaches of the Montaña, it is a matter for concern, and illustrates clearly the increasing mobility of the Indian population.

It is axiomatic, of course, that none of the inhabitants of the slums on stilts calls himself an Indian. In a small survey conducted with the (Fundamentalist) South American Indian Mission, which operates a center near this district, not

235

one person interviewed, no matter how barbarous his Spanish, accepted the term "Indian." The least urbanized admitted only to a recent move from Iquitos (far to the north), even though they were patently from tribes to the south of Pucallpa. But to acknowledge their Indian lineage—even to admit that they could speak their original tongue—was unbearable. For it brought back the stigma of being Indian; it brought back memories of being automatically cheated, lied to, browbeaten, of cruelties and indignities escaped, by and large, by fleeing to Pucallpa.

Other forces transform the Montaña Indian into a Peruvian. The State also molds him into the national image. Of its institutions, the schools may be discounted, since they touch only a very small fraction of the Indian population; and that fraction is in the two big cities. For despite the Peruvian law that guarantees a primary education to any child regardless of race, the Indians' drive for knowledge and education is throttled: the Indian child is not welcome in the back-country public schools and rarely manages to get in.

The Army, however, has much greater impact. Peru has universal military conscription, and in some areas, notably around Pucallpa and Iquitos, considerable numbers of Indians are drafted since they are within reasonable reach. Two years of military service will give an Indian a fairly fluent command of Spanish, "white" standards of dress and patterns of behavior; they may even make him semiliterate. (The Army has night courses for illiterates, but all a man may learn is his alphabet.) All this will transform the Montaña Indian into a Peruvian, and upon his discharge he will have an identity card to prove it. Even more powerful is the knowledge the Indian acquires in the Army: that there are means of getting redress from those who wrong him; and he can—at least in the two big cities—make use of them.

The State has other forces that impinge upon the Indian: the police and the Guardia Civil will casually impress any available Indian without an identity card to do chores around jails and barracks; the judicial and penal systems force him into Peruvian modes of conduct; the Servicio Sanitario and its malaria eradication program (probably the most far-flung arm of the State), will appear suddenly in the tiniest, most backwater hutment, with high-pressure DDT guns.

The protective arm of the State grows weaker the farther one goes from the two big cities, while the impact of the System grows correspondingly stronger. In remote villages and backwater compounds the process of Peruvianization is bitterly fought by the *patrones;* indeed the struggle has been going on in the Montaña ever since lay and cleric first met here. In 1884 the Peruvian explorer Samanez wrote that for the *patrones* "it is most convenient that the savages should retain . . . their absolute ignorance." This is almost as true today.

III

IN THE MONTAÑA TODAY, the great mass of tribalized Indians has no contact with either the cities or the missions. It is inevitable, however, that they will enter into the mainstream of Montaña society. And when they do, it seems equally inevitable that they will enter through processes that will produce their tribal death and their degradation as human beings.

Were we able today to identify all of the destructive and constructive forces at work during the process of acculturation, we might find ways of lessening the social costs involved. Yet all we can do at the present moment is to come up with partial solutions to bits and pieces of the larger problem. While we are not able today to assess so broad a problem as social costs, we can expect answers to such specific questions as determining the optimal time to bring a tribe into the dominant civilization; whether bilingual schools hold any real advantage over monolingual; the values (and deficits) of having Indians retain pride of tribe; which jungle products might find good markets, yet can be extracted through methods which do not reduce the Indian culturally.

Any group that wants to be of real assistance to technologically primitive people must be prepared to recognize that they will have to get professional help from such disciplines as ethnology, agronomy, sociology, and psychology: first to define the problems that confront these primitive people, and then to work out possible solutions.

Unfortunately, few groups are willing to seek such professional assistance. In the Montaña most Government agencies are too bound up in the framework of Peruvian society to be able to expand their operative horizons in this manner; Indians have no voice in either national or local policies. Most religious groups are utterly certain that theirs are the only valid programs for assisting the Indian, whether they aim at his total Peruvianization or total sequestration. Thus Father Marcelino of El Rosario Mission announced to Cornell Capa:

> [The Indians] have a right to have civilization, to perfect themselves, and nothing should stop them. It is a natural right, and we have an

obligation to teach them because we are more advanced.... We want them to assimilate to a more civilized life . . . to improve their way of life . . . obtain civilized things, to wear good clothes.

And he went on to compare his Order's work with that of the S.I.L., finding that his was "the road to assimilation; not the road to separation." The South American Indian Mission was equally unwilling to question its model of Reservation—the *noli me tangere* concept of sealing themselves off from outside evils.

Somewhere between these two poles lies the S.I.L., and it has got there because it is beginning to ask questions. Originally the group's fundamental program was concerned only with the establishment of bilingual schools, translation of the New Testament, and assistance in organizing native congregations. Yet even this limited program forced the S.I.L. to recognize that it was creating moral, spiritual, and ethical revolutions amongst the primitive people. What it did not realize until very recently was that its fundamental program bore no relation to the way in which an Indian earned his daily bread. And yet the way in which a man is forced to live significantly determines how much of a man he can become, both physically and psychologically.

It is only recently that the S.I.L. has come to realize that in order to maintain spiritual revolutions, it must also create socio-economic counterparts amongst the tribes. For the quite extraordinary accomplishments of the Lingüísticos over the past twenty years cannot gloss over the fact that as late as 1961, when Capa and I were in Peru, a large majority of the linguist fieldworkers were unwitting, frequently reluctant, and mostly unprepared revolutionaries. Yet we did find that a few of its members were trying to spell out what might be the objectives of a technological development program, and were searching for the means of implementing it. These were the Lingüísticos who had come to fear that Santos, the visionary bilingual schoolteacher with his futile dreams of transforming a wilderness, would come to typify the whole of the S.I.L. program. These members have been trying to expand S.I.L.'s horizons and have proposed that tribal workers include members trained in disciplines other than linguistics. Such a move gives rise to the hope that the S.I.L. may eventually develop into an institute of both spiritual and technical development.

An agency organized along these lines appears to offer the best hope to primitive people today. Because these societies are mostly found in countries which lack the resources and trained manpower to help even their own nationals, I am convinced that the survival—certainly the cultural survival—of primitive people will depend largely upon the efforts of groups like the S.I.L. whose motivating force drives them to the inhospitable and frequently unrewarding areas of the world. Whether the forces be Catholic or Protestant, Buddhist or Mohammedan, matters little so long as their mission involves more than the mere urge to proselytize a particular faith. Today's mission must equally involve the goal of searching out an economic and cultural identity for the primitive people in question.

"No society is fundamentally bad; all offer their members certain advantages," writes the great French ethnologist Lévi-Strauss. This is not an easy lesson to learn, especially for missionaries. Many, undoubtedly, will never come to accept it. Yet unless they do, they will see their efforts founder upon frustrations and resentments that they themselves will have created.

While I hold no particular brief for primitive cultures, I do believe that we bear the responsibility for assessing the respective advantages and disadvantages of cultures in conflict. And because we are the stronger by virtue of our technology, because we are the intruders in the world of primitive people, it is our responsibility to develop social policies to solve these problems. Much as it may dismay us, we are indeed our brother's keeper.

References Cited

Anderson, Lambert.
 Personal communications, 1961–1963.
Yarinacocha, Peru: Summer Institute of Linguistics.

Burroughs, William S.
 Naked lunch.
New York: Grove Press, 1959. XVI, 255 p.

Carneiro, Robert L.
 "The Amahuaca and the spirit world."
Ethnology, 3:6–11 (January 1964).

Cieza de Leon, Pedro.
 The Incas [ed. by Victor W. Von Hagen; transl. by Harriet de Onís].
Norman, Oklahoma: University of Oklahoma Press, 1959. LXXX, 397 p.

Dole, Gertrude.
 "Endocannibalism among the Amahuaca Indians."
New York Academy of Sciences. Transactions, Ser. II, vol. 68:567–573 (March 1962).

———.
 "The influence of population density on the development of social organization among the Amahuaca Indians of Eastern Peru."
Paper read before American Anthropological Association's Annual Meeting, Philadelphia, November 1961.

———.
 "Ownership and exchange among the Kuikuru Indians of Mato Grosso."
Revista do Museu Paulista, 10:125–133 (1956–1958).

———, and Robert L. Carneiro.
 Unpublished field notes on the Amahuaca, and personal communications, 1961–1964.
American Museum of Natural History, Department of Anthropology.

Great Britain. Parliament. House of Commons.
Papers by Command. Cd 6266.
 Correspondence respecting the treatment of British subjects and native Indians employed in the collection of rubber in the Putumayo district.
London: His Majesty's Stationery Office, July 1912 (Sessional Papers vol. 68 [February 1912 to March 1913]. Miscellaneous no. 8).

Harkness, Ruth.
 Pangoan diary.
New York: Creative Age, 1942. 295 p.

Izaguirre, Ispizúa, Padre Fray Bernardino, ed.
 Historia de las misiones franciscanas y narración de los progresos de la geografía en el oriente del Peru: relatos originales y producciones en lenguas indigenas de varios misioneros, 1619–1921.
Lima: Talleres tipográficos de la Penitenciaría, 1922–1929. 14 vols.

Ibid., vol. 1:269–274.
 "Salen los nuestros de San Miguel: Diario del Padre [Manuel] Biedma."

Ibid., vol. 8:229–255.
 "Carta y diario del Padre Fray Juan Dueñas, misionero del Colegio de Ocopa, agosto a septiembre, 1792."

Ibid., vol. 9:31–55.
 "Breve noticia del estado de las Misiones de Manoa en la Pampa del Sacramento, sus progresos y adelantemientos, con un discurso cronológico de sus naciones bárbaras, ríos, costumbres, y el estado en que se hallaban el año de 1820" [por Fray Jerónimo Leceta].

Ibid., vol. 9:308–325.
 "Gobierno del Padre Hermoso. Misión a los Amahuacas del Tamaya. Naufragio i muerte del P. Tapía. Sublevación de los indíjenes."

Ibid., vol. 9:313–328.
 "Viaje de los padres misioneros del Convento del Cuzco a las tribus salvajes de los Campos, Piros, Cunibos, y Sipibos en el año de 1874" [por Padre Fray Luis Sabaté].

Larrabure y Correa, Carlos, ed.
 Colección de leyes, decretos, resoluciones y otros documentos oficiales referentes al Departamento de Loreto.
Lima: Ministerio de Relaciones Exteriores, Tipografía del Estado, 1911. 18 vols. [Publicada Jefe del Archivo de Limites].

Ibid., vol. 11:369–588.
 "Diario de los viajes y exploración [de] los ríos Urubamba, Ucayali, Amazonas, Pachitea y Palcazú" [por Carlos Fry].

Ibid., vol. 11:254–369.
 "Exploración de los ríos Apurímac, Ene, Uru-

bamba y Ucayali" [por José B. Samanez Ocampo].

Lévi-Strauss, Claude.
  Tristes tropiques.
Paris: Plon, 1955. 462 p.

Marcoy, Paul [pseud.]
  Travels in South America from the Pacific Ocean to the Atlantic Ocean [by Laurent Saint-Cricq].
London: Blackie, 1875. 2 vols. [transl. from the French 2nd edition].

Morote Best, Efraín.
  "Tres temas de la selva."
Tradición, revista peruana de cultura (Cuzco), año 7, nos. 19–20: 59–70 (January 1957).

Nimuendaju, Curt.
  The Tukuna [ed. by Robert H. Lowie; transl. by William D. Hohenthal].
Berkeley, Calif.: University of California Press, 1952. IX, 210, XVIII p. (Univ. of Calif. Publications in American Archaeology and Ethnology, no. 45).

Patino Samudio, Manuel.
  "El caucho y la shiringa."
Sociedad Geográfica de Lima. Boletín, 11: 62–113 (January 1901).

Raimondy, Antonio.
  Apuntes sobre la provincia litoral de Loreto.
Lima: Tipografía Nacional, 1862. 190 p.

Russell, Robert.
  Unpublished notes and personal communications, 1953–1964.
Yarinacocha, Peru: Summer Institute of Linguistics.

Schurz, William L., et al.
  Rubber production in the Amazon valley.
Washington: U.S. Government Printing Office, 1925. VIII, 369 p. (Department of Commerce, Trade Promotion Series, no. 23).

Steward, Julian H., ed.
  Handbook of South American Indians.
Washington: U.S. Government Printing Office, 1946–1950. 7 vols. (U.S. Bureau of American Ethnology, Bulletin no. 143).

Valdez Lozano, Zacarías.
  La exploración del río Madre de Dios por Carlos Fermín Fitzcarrald.
Iquitos, Peru: Reategui, 1942.

Villanueva, Manuel Pablo.
  Fronteras de Loreto.
Sociedad Geográfica de Lima. Boletín, 12: 361–479 (December 1902); 13: 30–54 (January 1903).

Wallace, Alfred R.
  A narrative of travels on the Amazon and Rio Negro.
London: Reeve, 1853. VIII, 541, 1 p.

Guide to Pronunciation

A Spanish rendition of Amahuaca words has been followed to accord with the orthography developed by Robert Russell, linguist-missionary of the Summer Institute of Linguistics. In the belief that some of the tonal nuances are not apparent to English readers under his system, I have deviated somewhat from his forms. Thus, I use "w" when this represents the actual sound, rather than the Spanish "v."

      The following are approximate vowel values: "a" is pronounced as in far; "i," "y," as in feet; "u" as in hoot; "e" as in late; and "o" as in rope. A doubled vowel generally has the same tonal value as the single, except that it is slightly drawn out; two different vowels become a diphthong.

      The "j" is the explosive, back-of-the-throat Spanish "j," while "x" is the slurred Portuguese-Brazilian "x" that sounds like "sh"; "c" is a hard "k," except before "e" and "i," when it becomes "s" (the South American rather than Castillian pronunciation). In a number of cases I heard "b," "d," and "h" acting as "separators," although Russell would disagree with my including these letters in the actual spelling. In the pronunciation guide to Amahuaca proper names that follows, almost audible letters are indicated in parentheses, and accent marks indicate stress.

AMAHUACA PROPER NAMES IN TEXT

Amahuaca	A-ma-wá-ka	Munsho	Mun-shó
Coyaso	Ko-yá-so	Muxcaa Wundaa	Músh-ca(a) Wún-da(a)
Cuho	Kú-ho	Pacho	Pá-cho
Cunan Wahi	Kú-nan Wá-hi	Pansitimba	Pan-si-tím-(b)a
Iriya	I-rí-ya	Rohanhno	Ro-hán(h)n-o
Ishman	Ish-mán	Tumonno	Tú-mon(n)-o
Jawachiwayamba	Ha-wa-chi-wa-yám(b)-a	Wando	Wán-do
Mananyamba	Ma-nan-yám(b)-a	Winda	Wín(d)-a
Maswanhno	Mas-wán(h)n-o	Wocon	Wo-kón
Maxoopo	Ma-shó(o)-po	Yamba Wachi	Yám(b)-a Wá-chi